The
Lake Michigan
Triangle

THE LAKE MICHIGAN TRIANGLE

MYSTERIOUS DISAPPEARANCES AND HAUNTING TALES

GAYLE SOUCEK

THE
History
PRESS

Published by The History Press
Charleston, SC
www.historypress.com

Cover images: A Douglas C-54 Skymaster, the military transport aircraft later converted to commercial DC-4. *Wikimedia Commons*; a winter sunset shows a deceptively calm Lake Michigan, but its weather is known to change suddenly and with little warning; a summer storm rolls in over the north pier on Lake Michigan in Manitowoc; Lake Michigan's unpredictable waves can grow to massive heights; strange electrical or magnetic disturbances have been blamed for instrument failure in aircraft; as the sun drops below the horizon, the waters of the Lake Michigan Triangle are beautiful yet foreboding.

First published 2022

Manufactured in the United States

ISBN 9781467148399

Library of Congress Control Number: 2022937898

Notice: The information in this book is true and complete to the best of our knowledge. It is offered without guarantee on the part of the author or The History Press. The author and The History Press disclaim all liability in connection with the use of this book.

CONTENTS

INTRODUCTION

THE LAKE MICHIGAN TRIANGLE

The world, even the smallest parts of it, is filled with things you don't know.
—*Sherman Alexie, author*

Most people have heard of the Bermuda Triangle, the mysterious section of the Atlantic Ocean responsible for the unexplained disappearances of numerous ships and planes. It was first given its ominous name in a 1964 *Argosy* magazine article by Vincent Gaddis; it was later wildly popularized in a 1974 book by Charles Berlitz. What isn't as widely known is that there are dozens of such "triangle" areas around the world—many are much deadlier than their Atlantic counterpart. In fact, one of the deadliest lies in our own backyard: the Lake Michigan Triangle.

Although the origins of the name aren't clear, aviator Jay Gourley's 1977 book, *The Great Lakes Triangle*, began to weave together the tragic tales of strange shipwrecks, disappearances and plane crashes across the Great Lakes region. Later authors honed in on a rash of mysteries centered in Lake Michigan and described the Lake Michigan Triangle as an area bounded by Manitowoc, Wisconsin, to Ludington, Michigan, and down to Benton Harbor, Michigan. However, those boundaries only capture a small portion of the strange and unsettling happenings that span Lake Michigan's 22,404 square miles. Although the concept of a neat triangle aids the reader in clearly envisioning a specific area, tragedies aren't so easily confined to rigid geometric lines. For that reason, this book will contain some oddities and incidents that fall around the immediate shores of the lake and aren't just confined to its watery boundaries.

ABOUT THE LAKE

The Great Lakes are relative youngsters in geological history. They were formed about fourteen thousand years ago as retreating glaciers scraped along the land and created basins that filled with meltwater, but millions of years before the glaciers arrived, the area was actually an ancient Silurian tropical sea. Unequal erosion from that sea formed a prominent ridge of bedrock, known as the Niagara Escarpment, that partially encircles Lake Michigan. It begins in northern Illinois near the lake's western edge, hugs its northern border and stretches over Lake Huron east to New York, where its famous namesake waterfalls thrill spectators. Lake Michigan is considered the second-largest of the five Great Lakes by volume and the third-largest by surface area. You might be surprised, however, to learn that Lake Michigan and Lake Huron are really just one giant lake, connected hydrologically by the five-mile-wide Straits of Mackinac. Water flows between them, and they maintain the same water level. Viewed together, Michigan-Huron is the largest freshwater lake by surface area in the world. And although science tells us they're two lobes of one singular massive lake, legally and historically they've always been treated as separate entities.

But what makes Lake Michigan so deadly? More than one thousand drownings have occurred in the Great Lakes just since 2010, and more than half of those have been in Lake Michigan alone. Some of the factors are due to the elongated shape and position of the lake. Its shores are parallel and unobstructed, which contributes to the formation of dangerous currents, such as riptide and longshore tides, and the north–south orientation combines with normal wind patterns to churn waves to great heights. Rip currents and strong undertows make swimming extremely dangerous, and the massive and unpredictable waves can sweep pedestrians off piers or drag them from shorelines. It's those same waves that are blamed for many of the shipwrecks, either swamping the vessels or smashing them to bits on the rocky shoals that line the coast. And the water is cold! Winter water temperatures typically hover just above freezing, and the summer average is only about sixty-two degrees Fahrenheit, although it can get into the low seventies if conditions are just right in July. Hypothermia can occur in any water temperature below seventy degrees Fahrenheit (depending on length of exposure), so that means that most months of the year, the water temperature is a potential danger to swimmers. Since historical records have been kept, it's estimated that nearly 300,000 people have fallen to the ferocity of this lake, and nearly 10,000 ships have plummeted to its depths.

Surely, the inherent structural and environmental dangers of the lake are responsible for much of the death toll, but there are plenty of instances when natural explanations don't seem to fit—that's when we have to at least consider the possibility of the unnatural.

Magnetic Anomalies

One common theory blamed for "triangle" disappearances is that magnetic anomalies cause compasses to spin wildly and become ineffective. To put it simply, there are two main factors that affect compasses: magnetic declination (sometimes referred to as variation) and magnetic deviation. Declination is the difference between true north and magnetic north, and that varies from place to place around the globe. Mariners and pilots need to account for and adjust to these variations or they'll find themselves way off course. Lake Michigan, on average, varies about 4 to 5 degrees to the west, although there's a localized anomaly near Escanaba that varies by 13.8 degrees or more. Declination can change over time too, as it's affected by things such as erosion.

In recent years, there have been numerous reports of black sand on several Lake Michigan beaches. The unusually colored grains are mostly composed of magnetite, a magnetic mineral that's present in the igneous and metamorphic rocks that form the lake's basin and shoreline. The normal concentration of magnetite in Lake Michigan beach sand is about 2 percent, but measurements of up to 20 percent aren't uncommon when high water or strong wave action drag more of the particles to the shore. Although it's unlikely that these events cause significant or sudden changes in declination, it's an example of a natural process that can have an eventual impact.

Magnetic deviation, on the other hand, is the error induced in a compass by a nearby magnetic field. For example, if you were to hold a compass near a large hunk of iron, the needle would point to the iron, not to magnetic north. Plenty of common things produce a magnetic field, including many metals, electronics, power lines, batteries, cellphones, keys...even underwire bras! Of course, it's silly to think that a pilot's bra could cause the plane to crash or wind up off course, but potential magnetic deviation is a factor in navigation.

So, is it likely that magnetic anomalies are the cause of some triangle disasters? Probably not, but a deviation—say, from an electrical storm—could possibly cause a magnetic compass to act unpredictably. While that alone wouldn't be a major problem, especially in a commercial aircraft or ship with other sophisticated navigational equipment, it could certainly contribute to confusion in an inexperienced or inattentive pilot or mariner in smaller private vessels.

Ley Lines and Energy Vortexes

The concept of ley lines was first introduced in the 1920s by English antiquarian Alfred Watkins and later adopted by various groups such as the Earth mysteries movement, ufologists and other esoteric sects, each of which added its own spin. Originally, Watkins noticed that he could draw straight lines on a map that intersected with various ancient landmarks and structures. He thought that these represented early trade routes, but archaeologists summarily dismissed his theory, noting that it would have been impractical for primitive people to travel in a straight line that crossed mountains or waterways. In addition, they pointed out that it would be nearly impossible to draw a line across Britain that *didn't* cross over a few important archaeological sites, as the country is filled with them. Undeterred, in 1927, Watkins published a book titled *The Ley Hunter's Manual*. When he died in 1935, only a few proponents remained, and his theories were soon mostly forgotten—that is, until the counterculture movement of the 1960s.

At that point, the idea of ley lines enjoyed a renaissance of sorts, but with the added twist that the lines were thought to be imbued with some sacred significance or mystical power. These lines of power were believed to emanate ancient earth energies, somewhat akin to the idea of a geological feng shui. In places where ley lines cross, the intersection is said to emit still more concentrated energy, possibly even creating an energy vortex. Many earth-based and pagan practices incorporate earth energies. Some ufologists have even advanced the theory that the lines act as a sort of landing guide for UFOs, although that belief hasn't been widely accepted. Interestingly, according to ley line maps, one runs almost directly down the middle of Lake Michigan from north to south.

Energy vortexes (or vortices) are a more recent concept, one that can be traced to psychic Page Bryant. Bryant was self-described as "a teacher of sacred ecology and Earth healing," and while living in Sedona, Arizona, she advanced the idea that certain locations on earth either gave off or received sacred energy that could trigger healing and a higher consciousness. The *Visit Sedona* blog explains it: "[T]here are special spots that have been identified where the energy is more intense and where you are more likely to actually feel the energy. These vortexes have been further categorized into 'feminine' (energy entering the earth) and 'masculine' (energy coming out of the earth)....The vortex energy is powerful and transformational." Sites such as Stonehenge, the Great Pyramids of Egypt and the Mayan ruins in Mexico are considered to be vortexes, and believers stream there to tune into the spiritual energies. However, although vortexes are usually considered to be positive and healing, it's claimed that negative-energy vortexes exist as well. These points of powerful electromagnetic energy are believed to cause disharmony and potential danger.

Although there's no proof that ley lines or energy vortexes exist, they've been mentioned as possible explanations for mysterious happenings in places associated with energetic anomalies. Places like the Lake Michigan Triangle.

UNIDENTIFIED FLYING OR SUBMERGED OBJECTS (UFOS AND USOS)

This book would be remiss if it didn't include the most popular usual suspects for strange disappearances: UFOs and USOs (and UAPs, or unidentified aerial phenomena, the term most currently preferred by government agencies). Whatever you call them, these otherworldly visitors have been documented in our skies (and sometimes in our waters) since pre-biblical times. Originally, all UFO sightings were understood to mean extraterrestrials, and people who saw "spaceships" found themselves to be the subject of scorn and ridicule. In fact, many observers refused to report their sightings, knowing that they'd be called liars or considered to be crazy by their peers. To be sure, some accounts are outright hoaxes, while others are merely misidentified aircraft or natural phenomena. A surprisingly large percentage, however, are truly not able to be identified, at least with our current technology.

Over the last few years, several world governments, including that of the United States, have begrudgingly begun to admit that there's *something* out there that they can't explain. Now, that doesn't necessarily mean that E.T. is cruising our skies—it just means we honestly don't know. The craft typically don't have any control surfaces or means of propulsion that we can replicate or even fully understand. During Cold War years, the U.S. military feared it was the Soviets flying overhead. The Soviets also saw the invaders and feared it was the United States. Scientists have said that based on the number of planets in our galaxy alone—more than 100 billion—the odds would be nearly incalculable that ours is the only one with intelligent life. But does that mean they're contacting us?

Recently, a host of alternate explanations emerged, some less probable than others. One theory is that the visitors are not interstellar, but interdimensional, traveling through dimensions of time and space that are beyond our grasp. (On a side note, that's sometimes the explanation offered for the appearance of cryptids as well.) Another theory insists that they're intra-earth travelers, with bases constructed at the bottom of deep lakes and oceans or in subterranean stations carved into mountains. Of course, there's always the Hollow Earth theorists, and a more recent claim is that our government is hiding the fact that the moon is a secret space base, with entrances on the dark side so that the comings and goings won't be seen by earthlings.

Are UFOs to blame for missing planes and ships around Lake Michigan? There does seem to be an association between many of the incidents and the sightings of strange lights in the area, but it's pretty hard to blame something we can't even identify.

So, what does this all mean in relation to the disappearances and mysterious happenings in the Lake Michigan Triangle? Is there any explanation that fits? Unfortunately, no. It's possible that the truth lies somewhere in the middle of it all, between those who believe that everything has a natural explanation and those who wonder, "What if…?"

THE UNFRIENDLY SKIES

Luck is a very thin wire between survival and disaster,
and not many people can keep their balance on it.
—*Hunter S. Thompson, American journalist and author*

F ear of flying is a pretty common phobia. Even the most seasoned
traveler sometimes experiences "white-knuckle" flights, when bad
weather and terrible turbulence combine to make it feel like the
aircraft will surely rattle itself to pieces. But perhaps surprisingly, air travel is
an extremely safe undertaking. According to the National Safety Council
(NSC), you're 95 times more likely to die from accidental poisoning. And
while you have a 1 in 1.9 million chance of being blasted to oblivion by
a lightning bolt or a 1 in 5.5 million chance of being assassinated by an
angry bee, the odds of dying in a plane crash on a U.S. commercial flight
are about 1 in 11 million. And no, that's not a typo. There's an old joke
passed around flight schools that says the most dangerous part of flying is
driving to the airport. Since the lifetime odds of being killed in a car crash
hover around 1 in 101, you're definitely safer flying to your destination
instead of taking a road trip.

Of course, planes do sometimes crash, and the resulting loss of life is always
heartbreaking. In most cases, the National Transportation Safety Board
(NTSB) is able to pinpoint the exact cause after a careful and exhaustive
investigation and recommend changes to flight procedures or to the aircraft
type itself to prevent future incidents. Its predecessor, the Civil Aeronautics

Board (CAB), handled investigations before 1967. But what happens when there is no clearly defined cause? What happens when a perfectly sound aircraft falls from the sky, or an experienced flight crew makes unexplainable decisions with tragic results? Those are the times when we can only wonder what unforeseen forces may have tipped the hand of fate.

THE MYSTERIOUS DISAPPEARANCE OF FLIGHT 2501

The evening of June 23, 1950, was warm and humid at LaGuardia Airport, with a gentle breeze out of the south. Not as uncomfortable as the sweltering weather that was yet to come midsummer, but those rushing to catch a flight would have appreciated the relatively cooler temperatures inside the airport's grand terminal. It was a busy time for commercial aviation; LaGuardia was handling more than two hundred flights per day, and that number was increasing rapidly. That evening, Northwest Orient Airlines Flight 2501 was not a regularly scheduled flight, but rather had been added to the schedule to accommodate those passengers who had been unable to secure a seat on the fully booked Flight 501, daily service from New York to Seattle with stops in Detroit, Milwaukee, Minneapolis, Billings and Spokane. Flight 2501 was flying a slightly abbreviated route, stopping only in Minneapolis and Spokane, but it was also fully booked. When it rumbled onto the runway just past 7:30 p.m. to prepare for departure, with 2,500 gallons of fuel and a full load of passengers and luggage, it was a mere fifty-eight pounds under its maximum allowable takeoff weight.

Nevertheless, the DC-4, tail no. N95425, was equipped with four powerful Pratt & Whitney R-2000 Twin Wasp engines. The massive fourteen-cylinder radial engines were originally developed to power military aircraft and could generate up to 1,450 horsepower at 2,700 rpm. In fact, this particular plane had begun its life as a C-54A Skymaster, built for the U.S. Army Air Forces by Douglas Aircraft in 1943. In late 1945, the government sold off surplus equipment, and several hundred Skymasters were converted to civilian use. This was one of forty in the Northwest fleet, and it had enough fuel on board to fly for about eleven hours, well more than a respectable safety margin for its six-hour flight. And although a preflight review of the weather showed a line of thunderstorms and possible squalls between New York and Minneapolis, it wasn't of great concern for the flight crew. It would likely be very bumpy—and passengers hated turbulence—but there was nothing to fear. Still, with an eye toward passenger comfort, Captain Robert

Lind requested approval to fly at four thousand feet instead of his assigned altitude of six thousand feet. He hoped that staying mostly below the cloud line would make the trip a bit smoother. His request was denied due to other traffic at that altitude.

When the aircraft neared Cleveland, Ohio, just before 10:00 p.m., Lind decided to repeat his request, and this time it was approved. Cleveland Air Traffic Control instructed the pilot to descend to four thousand feet and maintain that altitude. By this hour, most of the passengers were probably asleep in the darkened cabin as the DC-4 plowed uneventfully through the night sky. They would have no idea of the disaster that loomed before them.

At that time, flights at night, or those operating in poor visibility, relied on a system of low-frequency radio range (LFR) navigation to stay on course. The ingenious system was designed by British engineer Frank Adcock to create virtual lanes in the sky and keep aircraft safely separated. It consisted of hundreds of stations across the country, usually spaced about two hundred miles apart, each consisting of four equidistant antenna towers that could transmit or receive directional radio waves. Some busier stations added a fifth tower in the center for voice transmission. By tuning into a station's specified AM radio frequency, the pilots would hear a series of Morse code signals, transmitting the letters "A" and "N." If they just heard the code for "N," they needed to turn slightly to the left; if they heard only the code for "A," they needed to turn slightly right. When the signals blended into a continuous tone, they were right on track. This system stayed in use until the 1950s, when it was gradually replaced by very high-frequency omni-directional range (VOR), which fed information to instruments in the cockpit. And now, in the twenty-first century, ground VOR stations are being decommissioned in favor of satellite-based GPS. However, on that stormy night in 1950, Captain Lind and his copilot, Verne Wolfe, would have been very busy monitoring the LFR to keep their aircraft on course.

As Flight 2501 headed for its next checkpoint of Battle Creek, Michigan, the captain of a Lockheed Lodestar flying over Lake Michigan reported severe turbulence that had tossed his plane so violently that he had lost 500 feet in altitude. Air Traffic Control (ATC) realized that the Lodestar would eventually be passing directly over the DC-4. In order to maintain a safe margin of separation in the storm, the controller on duty instructed Captain Lind to descend to 3,500 feet. He was only too happy to oblige. The towering clouds and gusty winds made controlling the bulky aircraft tiring, and he hoped that a lower altitude might avoid some of the worst choppiness.

At some point, Lind and Wolfe made the decision to steer south in an attempt to fly around some of the worst storm activity. What the flight crew didn't know was that they were heading right into a menacing line of squalls that stretched nearly three hundred miles north and south; there was no way to bypass it. The captain could have decided to turn around and take temporary shelter at another airport en route and wait for the storm to pass, but he was mindful of the inconvenience this would cause for the passengers and the added expense for his employer. Besides, he really didn't have any concerns for safety. The storm was an annoyance and one that was making the flight unpleasant and bumpy, but there was nothing to fear. The aircraft was well built to withstand the stresses of the weather, and numerous other flights were safely navigating the treacherous weather that night. Soon they'd be on the ground in Minneapolis—their home base—where another crew would relieve them for the remainder of the flight. Lind probably looked forward to climbing into his own bed for a good night's sleep.

At 11:13 p.m., Flight 2501 made one last radio transmission, requesting clearance to descend to 2,500 feet. They gave no reason for their request, but it's likely that the crew was attempting to drop below the clouds and perhaps gain some visual perspective by sighting the lights of the towns along the shoreline. Although they had been handed off by Cleveland to the Chicago ATC, the aircraft was in the vicinity of Benton Harbor, Michigan, and was due to pass over Milwaukee around 11:37 p.m. However, due to some departing aircraft on the ground at Milwaukee, Chicago ATC was unable to grant the change of altitude. The crew acknowledged the denial. That was the last that anyone would hear from Flight 2501.

Shortly thereafter, numerous residents of the many small towns between Benton Harbor and South Haven would report hearing a very low-flying plane along the Lake Michigan shoreline before seeing a brilliant flash of light over the lake. Some reported the sound of an explosion—although it was hard to tell for certain amid the booming thunder and blinding lightning—but none of this was relayed to authorities at the time. Just before midnight, Northwest radio operatives at Mitchell Field in Milwaukee radioed the DC-4, requesting a position report; the aircraft should have reported in by then. There was no answer from the plane. Now greatly concerned, they instructed the pilot to circle the range station at Madison, Wisconsin, in case his radio had merely failed. At the same time, all CAA (Civil Aeronautics Administration, the predecessor to the FAA) radio stations began broadcasting on all frequencies between Chicago and Minneapolis in the hopes of raising a response. As radio operators across the region listened nervously and the tower personnel anxiously scanned the sky with binoculars to no avail, it became clear that Flight 2501 was missing. Almost immediately, the CAA informed all air-sea rescue stations of the situation, including the air force, Coast Guard, navy and state police. By 5:30 a.m., any possible remaining hope had faded, as the potential maximum flight time of the DC-4—based on the amount of fuel on board—passed. When dawn broke, the search for the missing airliner began in earnest.

The Coast Guard cutter *Woodbine* was the first to confirm the disaster. The crew discovered an oil slick and bits of debris about eighteen miles northwest of Benton Harbor, including the aircraft's logbook. Over the next few days, the search turned up more gruesome reminders of the lives lost. Captain C.G. Bowman of the ice cutter *Mackinac* reported that his men found "hands, ears, a seat armrest, and pieces of upholstery." A child's pants were later identified as belonging to eight-year-old Chester Schaeffer, who was on the flight with his mother. There was more: a chunk of skull about the size of a half dollar; a section of human spine; unidentified pieces of flesh; and a passenger's checkbook, with the last entry to Northwest Orient for payment of tickets for Flight 2501. In fact, the debris washing ashore in Michigan was so plentiful and heart-rending that officials temporarily closed some beaches along the shoreline.

But what caused the crash? Based on the evidence recovered, it appears that the aircraft hit the water at a very high velocity and in a forward, downward, slightly-to-the-left trajectory. Some theorized that lightning struck the plane and ignited the fuel tanks or that turbulence caused twisting of the fuselage, resulting in a spark. Although many residents of the area reported hearing an explosion, there was no indication of fire on any of the wreckage, which casts doubt on the theory that it exploded midair. The sound they heard was probably the craft striking the water. There was no obvious sign of mechanical failure on the recovered parts. A Douglas Aircraft Company investigator believed it was likely that the combination of severe wind, turbulence and the pilots' inability to establish a visual reference in the storm caused the DC-4 to flip over and become inverted; it had happened before in eight previous instances, but those pilots had each been at higher altitudes and were able to recover position without harm. At low altitude and likely disoriented, Lind and Wolfe didn't have that luxury of time. Others believed that the aircraft had been taken by UFOs, a theory that gained some traction when two police officers in Michigan reported seeing strange red lights hovering over the lake about two hours after the flight reportedly went down. And although there was plenty of debris, searchers have never located any large pieces of the plane or its engines, despite numerous attempts. As of today, it is still undiscovered, although the Michigan Shipwreck Research Association has picked up the search and hopes that modern technology will eventually provide some answers.

In the end, the Civil Aeronautics Board closed its accident investigation at the time with the following terse statement: "The board determines that there is not sufficient evidence upon which to make a determination of probable cause." For the families and friends of the fifty-five passengers and three crew members who lost their lives, they would spend the remainder of their years wondering why their loved ones fell victim to the ravages of the Lake Michigan Triangle.

UNITED AIRLINES FLIGHT 389'S FLIGHT INTO THE WAVES

Just as the Northwest Orient Flight 2501 discussed previously had done fifteen years earlier, United Airlines Flight 389 prepared to depart LaGuardia Airport in New York on a warm, humid summer evening. It was August 16, 1965, and twenty-four passengers and six crewmembers climbed aboard the new, state-of-the-art Boeing 727-100 jetliner. These jets were designed specifically for short- to medium-range routes, and due to its sleek wing design, it was able to fly out of smaller airports with shorter runways. Its high-speed cruising capability, even at low altitudes, provided a fast and economical way to travel. With a top speed of 632 miles per hour and a reputation for stability, it quickly became one of the best-selling jets in commercial aviation history.

Flight 389 was a routine scheduled flight between New York and Chicago's O'Hare Airport, but the travelers on that route would fly in style; tail no. N7036U was only about two months old, and its three powerful Pratt & Whitney JT8D-1 engines should ensure a safe and speedy trip. The weather along the route was pleasant enough. There were high clouds and overcast skies, but there was little reported turbulence and no evidence of storm activity in the area. Visibility over Lake Michigan was reported at about seven miles beneath a ten-thousand-foot ceiling, with light winds of four knots (less than five miles per hour). At 7:52 p.m., Captain Melville W. Towle, an experienced pilot with more than seventeen thousand flight hours, advanced the throttle and sped down the runway for what promised to be an uneventful evening. And for most of the trip, it was.

Flying alongside Captain Towle that night were First Officer Roger Marshall Whitezell and Second Officer Maurice L. Femmer, along with three stewardesses: Phyllis M. Rickert, Sandra H. Fuhrer and Jeneal G. Beaver. ("Stewardess" was the official job title at the time; it has long since been changed to "flight attendant.") Such a short flight wouldn't have included meal service, but the passengers presumably enjoyed complimentary drinks and snacks as the miles ticked by. At 9:02 p.m., Flight 389 came under the control of Chicago Air Traffic Control and reported flight level 350. For reference, altitudes above eighteen thousand feet are reported as three-digit flight levels, so FL 350 referred to a cruising altitude of thirty-five thousand feet. Chicago ATC acknowledged and, at 9:03 p.m., directed the pilot to begin a descent to twenty-four thousand feet. UAL 389 replied, "…down to 240, leaving three-five." Moments later, controllers advised the flight to continue descending to an altitude of fourteen thousand feet. As the aircraft approached O'Hare's control zone, ATC sent one final instruction: continue descent to six thousand feet and change radio frequency to contact Chicago Approach Control (ORD) directly. Again the 727 acknowledged and repeated back the instructions. They immediately made contact with ORD as instructed, and Approach Control confirmed that they had the flight on radar. The crew was directed to set up for an instrument approach on O'Hare's runway 14R. Although it was standard procedure to utilize instrument approaches at night, the visibility was good enough that evening to allow the pilots visual contact with the runway lights. The pilot of a Boeing 707 that was about thirty miles behind the UAL flight later stated that once he broke through the clouds over Lake Michigan at about eight thousand to ten thousand feet, he could see lights on shore. His first officer added that although it was a bit hazy, he could see the water below clearly.

With only a few moments left in flight, the passengers on UAL 389 would have been expectantly readying themselves for arrival. Seat belts fastened, tray tables up and the stewardesses belted into jump seats, the pilot radioed "Roger!" to acknowledge final landing instructions. But just seconds later, a lifeguard at Chicago's North Avenue Beach House reported seeing a brilliant orange flash on the horizon as he strolled along the deserted beach, which was followed closely by a thunderous roar. While police and Coast Guard facilities began to be inundated with calls of an extraordinary explosion over Lake Michigan, Chicago Approach realized that Flight 389 had suddenly disappeared from radar.

In the terminal, O'Hare's Gate E-3 had earlier been filled with happy friends and family members waiting to welcome home the incoming passengers, but now it sat empty as they were quietly hustled into a plush red-carpeted waiting room off the gate. While they sat in shock and bewilderment, a somber representative from United Airlines, dressed sharply in the company's signature blue uniform, gently broke the news that the plane was "missing" and presumed down. Throughout the concourse and operational areas, United employees struggled to maintain composure as they contemplated the loss of their colleagues and the inevitable fear that they might someday face the same fate. "There but for the grace of God…" perhaps haunted their thoughts. In sharp contrast, groups of passengers arriving and departing on other flights, unaware of the tragedy unfolding around them, chatted cheerfully among themselves.

Almost immediately, an informal search team assembled at the North Shore Yacht Club in Highland Park, a waterfront town roughly twenty miles from O'Hare. Dozens of volunteer divers and private boaters headed out to search for survivors, while helicopters from Glenview Naval Air Station dropped phosphorus flares on tiny parachutes to illuminate the scene. They found plenty of twisted metal, hunks of fiberglass and ragged pieces of upholstery bobbing in the gentle waves, but no immediate sign of any passengers. By daylight, it had become devastatingly clear that there was no one alive to save. The formal recovery effort started in earnest that morning with Coast Guard and navy vessels, along with investigators from the Civil Aeronautics Board's Bureau of Aviation Safety. The search would ultimately last nearly a year and cost more than $500,000 as chartered boats combed the lake bottom, probing the mud and sand for the jet's "black box," the flight data recorder, which they hoped would provide some clue to the reason for the disaster. Although they eventually recovered all of the bodies, and a little more than 80 percent of the aircraft—including the mounting brackets for the black box—the recorder itself was never found.

Without the critical data that device would provide, speculation began to emerge. Some thought that the plane had exploded in midair, either due to sabotage or some inherent flaw in the design. Boeing stock fell as the company tried to defend itself against rumors, and the CAA even considered grounding all 727s until they could establish a probable cause. Some believed that a UFO had made the aircraft's avionics malfunction. Others even wondered if the pilot in command had intentionally flown into the water as a means of suicide. In the end, although investigators couldn't prove what had happened, they began to formulate a theory.

After examining the debris, they concluded that the plane had struck the water at a nose-up, slightly right-wing-down attitude, in clean flight configuration. The landing gear was fully retracted, and the flaps weren't yet extended for landing. There was no indication of fire before the 727 collided with the waves, and the last radio transmission, mere seconds before the crash, showed no sign of any problem. That seemed to point to the likelihood that the pilots were in normal flight with no obvious emergency or loss of control. In other words, three experienced pilots—in clear weather with decent visibility—had flown a nearly brand-new and perfectly functional aircraft directly into the foreboding and dark waves of Lake Michigan, killing themselves and all on board, for no apparent reason. But why?

Some clues soon began to emerge. At the time, the U.S. Air Force Air Defense Command was tasked with monitoring the skies for any incoming threats, such as Soviet missiles. It combined radar tracking along with a system of networked computers know as SAGE, or Semi-Automatic Ground Environment. Although it didn't specifically track commercial flights, SAGE provided a sort of three-dimensional picture of U.S. airspace at all times, should NORAD (North American Aerospace Defense Command) need to respond to a possible attack. The CAB investigators were able to obtain SAGE data from that night and identify UAL 389, and what they found was chilling. The first altitude reading of the flight was recorded at 9:14 p.m. and showed the plane at 16,500 feet; this was consistent with the controller's instructions for the pilots to begin a descent from 24,000 to 14,000 feet. However, at 9:19 p.m., about the time the pilot had received clearance to descend to 6,000 feet, SAGE data showed that the 727 was only at an altitude of 2,000 feet. It became clear to investigators that the flight crew had misread their altitude by 10,000 feet! They apparently believed they were at 12,000 feet and needed to descend to 6,000; in reality, they were already dangerously close to the forbidding waves. Seconds later, they struck the water, and the aircraft exploded on impact.

How could three experienced aviators in the cockpit all make such a simple but deadly mistake? Investigators turned their attention to the altimeter on the control panel. The 727 had two: one on the panel in front of the pilot and one in front of the copilot. Both devices operated independently from each other, using atmospheric pressure readings from a static port outside the aircraft to provide altitude. The model in use was a three-pointer design, looking similar to a clock face, in which a long pointer indicates hundreds of feet, a shorter diamond-shaped pointer indicates thousands of feet and the shortest pointer, which is cross-shaped, indicates ten thousands of feet. Although it was commonly in use at the time, that model of altimeter was more difficult to read and sometimes led to errors. The CAB suspected that an improper altitude reading by the crew lead to the disaster, but it left many questions unanswered. Even if one crew member misread the instrument, why didn't one of the other two notice the error? After all, the Boeing 707 crew following behind them stated that they could clearly see the water below. Why hadn't they realized from other visual cues, such as the lights onshore, that they were much lower than they thought? Even at night, that difference should have been obvious. They also had weather reports stating that the cloud ceiling was at about ten thousand feet. If they believed they were at twelve thousand feet, didn't it strike them as odd that they had been out of the clouds for several minutes?

Of course, this is all second-guessing what the actual crew members saw and believed that dreadful evening. Was it a misunderstood altimeter or something much darker and more mysterious? The CAB's final report simply stated, "The Board is unable to determine the reason for the aircraft not being leveled off at its assigned altitude of 6,000 feet." It was just another unsolved tragedy in the ominous, frigid waters of Lake Michigan.

THE FINAL FLIGHT OF A BEECHCRAFT BONANZA

May 12, 2019, was a routine day trip for pilot Randal Dippold and his passenger, Emanuel Z. "EZ" Manos. Together, they'd made the same flight many times before, including four trips over the past several weeks. Manos was president of the Detroit Salt Company, which operates a large salt mine in the middle of Detroit. It's a major supplier of bulk road salt in the Midwest and an important employer in the economically depressed city. He was also a successful entrepreneur and had purchased the Caledonia Native Copper Mine near Ontonagon, Michigan, in the Upper Peninsula of Michigan. The mine, which had begun operations in 1863, was largely dormant when Manos formed Evergreen Explorations, LLC, to purchase the property and open it to tourist "prospectors," who can spend the day panning for copper nuggets in a sluice or breaking rocks in an ore pile in search of copper, quartz, silver and other native minerals. With such far-flung business pursuits, Manos needed a quick way to travel between his home in Monroe, just south of Detroit, and far northern reaches of the Upper Peninsula. Purchasing a small plane made good business sense.

Randal Dippold was an experienced pilot, certified aircraft mechanic and flight instructor. He owned and operated Airservice Enterprise Inc. at the Livingston County Airport in Howell, Michigan, where the airplane, a single-engine Beechcraft V35 Bonanza registered to Evergreen Explorations, was hangared. Dippold frequently ferried Manos between his home in Monroe and the mine in Ontonagon. At the same time, he was teaching him to fly. It was an easy way to combine business with pleasure.

On that cloudy and unseasonably cool spring afternoon, the Bonanza departed Howell just before 4:00 p.m. and flew on a northwest heading to Ontonagon County–Schuster Field, arriving at 5:57 p.m. Whatever business Manos had at the mine, it didn't take long—they were on the ground for less than forty-five minutes. By 6:40 p.m. they were back in the air. Although it was overcast with occasional light rain, visibility was about ten miles, which was entirely suitable for flying under visual flight rules. It didn't really matter, however, as Dippold had a license rating that allowed him to fly under instrument-only conditions, and he was also certified as a flight instrument instructor. Although they didn't file a flight plan that day, after their short trip to Ontonagon, they were headed back to Custer Airport in Monroe, near Manos's home. Unfortunately, it's not clear whether Dippold had flown from Howell to Monroe earlier that day to pick up Manos or if they had met at the Howell airport; that would be an important missing clue in the later accident investigation.

FlightAware, a flight tracking service that provides aircraft position updates and other data, indicated that the airplane was at an altitude of 7,000 feet and traveling 160 miles per hour over Lake Michigan when, at 7:42 p.m., the pilot radioed Minneapolis Air Route Traffic Control Center (ARTCC) to report an emergency. The engine had suddenly failed, and the plane was now gliding helplessly without power over the water. ARTCC responded immediately, giving Dippold the locations and distances of the two nearest airports; it would be up to him to decide which he had the most favorable chance of reaching. He requested a heading to Frankfort Dow Memorial Field and said that he had the shoreline in sight. Under normal conditions, a Beechcraft Bonanza can glide for about 1.7 miles for each 1,000 feet in altitude above mean sea level. Under the circumstances, that meant they had roughly 10 miles to find land before gravity exacted its revenge. They had been cleared to land at Dow, and the pilot acknowledged and requested emergency equipment to be on hand in case of a rough or short landing. It certainly seemed like they would make it. In a final communication with ARTCC at 7:47 p.m., he reported that he was at 1,800 feet. Then…deadly radio silence. However, FlightAware continued tracking the aircraft for another two minutes, showing its last position about four miles west of the airport and only at 700 feet in altitude.

Almost immediately—probably before the plane even hit the water—the U.S. Coast Guard was notified and launched a search-and-rescue mission. Although it knew approximately where the aircraft had gone down from radar tracking, rescuers could find no trace of the Bonanza or any survivors. Oddly, the plane's emergency locator transmitter, which is a battery-powered transponder that is activated by the excessive G-forces experienced during a crash, did not activate. It's possible that Dippold landed the plane so gently on the water's surface that the device wasn't triggered. In that case, it would be likely that there was enough time for both men to exit safely. Although there's no standard calculation for how long an aircraft will float, one that isn't severely damaged by the water landing will usually remain afloat for at least several seconds up to several minutes, allowing the occupants time to escape. A sample of 179 water ditchings reported by the NTSB showed a survival rate of nearly 90 percent. Unfortunately, Dippold and Manos faced an even greater danger that day. According to nearby buoy readings, the water temperature was only between thirty-nine and forty-two degrees Fahrenheit. Without survival gear, hypothermia would set in quickly. Although a person could theoretically survive up to two hours in such cold water, lethargy and loss of muscle control would happen much sooner, making it impossible to swim or tread water.

After two fruitless days, the initial search ended. On May 22, the Michigan State Police Marine Services Team deployed a remotely operated underwater vehicle (ROV) and finally located the Bonanza at a depth of 540 feet. Video showed it to be in relatively good condition, with just some damage to the starboard wing. Eerily, the door was open, and no one was inside. The two men had escaped, but where were they? It took several more days of searching, but Manos's body was eventually located about 125 feet from the sunken plane; he had drowned. Dippold, however, was never found.

The discovery raised more questions than it answered. Why had the engine failed? There's some speculation that the "failure" was actually fuel starvation, but without knowing exactly where the plane had flown that day, it's impossible to know for certain. If it had flown with a full tank from Howell to Ontonagon, it would have had more than enough fuel to safely return to Monroe. If, however, it had first flown from Howell to pick up Manos at Monroe and then back to Howell before continuing on its journey, there wouldn't have been enough fuel on board. Small aircraft flying under visual flight rules to small airports—those without control towers—don't have to file flight plans or check in in any manner, so there's no record of any previous possible flight that day. But why would an experienced pilot like Dippold, flying with a conscientious student pilot like Manos, have made such a careless error?

Aside from the engine failure, why wasn't the aircraft able to glide safely to the nearby airport? The pilot had land in sight when he spoke with ARTCC. With visibility that day of ten miles and a calculated glide range of slightly more than ten miles, he should have reached the airport or at least come very close. Of course, there are other factors that can reduce glide, such as wind speed and direction, but the winds were very light that day, coming from the northwest, and shouldn't have impacted the flight. Why did the plane end up more than four miles from shore? And why didn't the Coast Guard find the pilots if they had indeed exited the plane before it sank? The rescuers were on the scene so quickly that it would seem that they would have found survivors.

In the end, the NTSB had no answers to these questions either. The probable cause statement read, "The National Transportation Safety Board determines the probable cause(s) of this accident to be: A loss of engine power for reasons that could not be determined based on the available information."

That's likely cold comfort to the wife, four children and twelve grandchildren of Randal Dippold, who have never had the closure of at least retrieving their loved one's body for a proper burial. Sometimes Lake Michigan just refuses to give up its prey.

DOGFIGHT WITH A UFO

Although this incident occurred just north of Lake Michigan over Lake Superior, it began at Kinross Air Force Base, an Air Defense Command base located on the Upper Peninsula of Michigan, directly between the two lakes. At about 6:00 p.m. on the cold, snowy and stormy night of November 23, 1953, Ground Intercept radar operators spotted an unidentified object flying in restricted air space near the Soo Locks, a crucial water link between Lake Superior, the lower Great Lakes and the Atlantic Ocean. Because more than 90 percent of the world's iron ore passes through these locks, it's a critical transportation route for both commercial and defense purposes and a promising target for our enemies. This was during the height of the Cold War, so any unknown aircraft in U.S. skies triggered a rapid response, especially one sighted in such a vulnerable area.

At that time, an F-89C Scorpion jet from Truax Air Force Base in Madison, Wisconsin, was on temporary assignment at Kinross, and it was immediately scrambled to intercept. First Lieutenant Felix Eugene Moncla Jr. was at the controls, with Second Lieutenant Robert L. Wilson acting as the Scorpion's radar operator. Wilson was having some difficulty maintaining track of the target, which seemed to dart rapidly around the airspace, so the ground operators provided directions to guide them toward the intruder. At about eight thousand feet, Moncla reported that he was closing in on the unknown aircraft, and ground control watched intently as the two blips on their screen drew closer together. Suddenly, the two targets merged into one. That can happen momentarily if one aircraft flies directly above or below the other, but the signals will immediately diverge again as the planes move apart. That didn't happen. As they watched in dismay, only the single unidentified blip moved across the screen on its original course, until it veered suddenly and disappeared in a burst of speed. An official report would later note that the F-89's radar signal had simply vanished when the blips converged. The controllers tried desperately to contact Moncla, but there was no response—only the staticky crackle of radio silence.

Almost immediately, search-and-rescue teams from both the U.S. Air Force and the Royal Canadian Air Force (RCAF) took to the skies in search of their missing comrades, but there was no sign of either the Scorpion or its intended target. It made no sense. If there had been a midair collision, it's unlikely that the other craft would have been able to remain in flight. If there was some sort of emergency, why hadn't Moncla or Wilson radioed for help? All transmissions had been normal up until the radar dots converged. What had they been chasing? And what happened when they approached? After days of extensive searches by both boat and aircraft and ground searches along the lake coastline, the rescuers finally admitted defeat. Not a single trace has ever been found of the jet or its occupants.

In the ensuing weeks, the U.S. Air Force floated several theories about what had occurred. At first, it claimed that the unidentified target had been an RCAF C-47 Skytrain that had flown off course, a claim that both the RCAF and the Skytrain pilot vigorously denied. Of course, that still wouldn't explain the Scorpion's disappearance. Some theorized that Moncla had experienced vertigo and had simply spun his craft into the lake, but there was certainly no indication to support that, and it still wouldn't explain the lack of debris.

Interestingly, Donald Keyhoe, a U.S. Marine Corps naval aviator and UFO investigator, later claimed that he had received a phone call from a U.S.

Air Force source on the night of the incident, who told him that the jet had collided with a UFO. Of course, the air force denied the claim, but it couldn't seem to come up with a consistent story. Moncla's widow was once told that her husband's plane exploded at high altitude; another representative told her that Moncla flew too low and into the water. Oddly, investigators from the National Investigations Committee on Aerial Phenomena (NICAP) found that apparently all records of that night's mission were removed from official records. When they reached out to the Aerospace Technical Intelligence Center, officials at the center claimed, "There is no record in the Air Force files of any sighting at Kinross AFB on November 23, 1953.... There is no case in the files which even closely parallels these circumstances." For a case that didn't exist, however, the air force went to a lot of trouble to investigate. Its own Project Blue Book group was deeply involved in the aftermath and later published a report claiming that the initial radar target was the Canadian C-47, the strange radar readings were due to a weather anomaly and Moncla simply got dizzy and crashed his jet into the dark, cold waters of the lake. For his part, Keyhoe accused the U.S. government of engaging in a conspiracy to cover up knowledge of flying saucers.

Was the Scorpion and its crew taken aboard a flying saucer? There was one other odd detail that emerged that night. A search-and-rescue pilot testifying before the USAF Accident Investigation Board said that he'd heard a brief radio transmission from the missing pilot about forty-five minutes *after* the plane had vanished. Could he be mistaken? Of course. But what if he's not?

The Transplant Tragedy

The heroes who operate organ transplant teams face life and death every day, but they know that the tragedy of one person's demise often means the gift of life for others. Sadly, on one fateful day over Lake Michigan, only death prevailed.

Just before 4:00 p.m. on Monday, June 4, 2007, a Cessna 550 Citation II took off from Milwaukee's General Mitchell Airport en route to Willow Run Airport near Ypsilanti, Michigan. It carried a precious cargo: a pair of lungs destined for a critically ill patient at a University of Michigan hospital. On board were pilot Bill Serra, First Officer Dennis Hoyes, transplant surgeons Dr. Martin Spoor and Dr. David Ashburn and transplant specialists Richard Chenault II and Rick LaPensee. At the other end of the flight, the patient lay waiting on the operating table, prepped and ready to receive the lifesaving organs. Only the very sickest individuals receive transplants, and the wait for a suitable donor can be long—oftentimes longer than the patient can survive. In fact, according to statistics, seventeen people in the United States die every day while waiting for a transplant that never comes; this patient was one of the "lucky" ones.

Earlier that day, the Michigan hospital had been notified of the donor in Milwaukee. Due to the extreme speed and precision required in coordinating the dual surgeries, the transplant team usually moved by helicopter, but for flights of more than two hundred miles, a helicopter wasn't practical. For that reason, the University of Michigan Health System in Ann Arbor leased the small business jet and contracted with Marlin Air to pilot and maintain it. That morning, the aircraft left Ypsilanti for the first leg of its mission at 11:00 a.m. and headed to Milwaukee on an uneventful flight. Once there, the medical transport team rushed to the hospital, while the pilots remained at the airport and ate lunch. Other pilots who spoke with them said that they appeared relaxed and in good spirits and spoke of acquiring more aircraft for Marlin. At around 3:30 p.m., the surgeons returned to the airport with the life-saving organs, and the team readied for takeoff.

There was a light rain falling over Milwaukee that afternoon, but nothing that would interfere with the flight. Serra was given clearance to depart on runway 1L, with instructions to climb to two thousand feet and then execute a right turn to the northeast. According to the cockpit voice recorder that was later recovered, seconds after they became airborne, the pilot asked the copilot, "Why am I fighting the controls here?…What the [expletive]'s going on? I'm fighting the controls…she's rolling on me. Help me, help me." One minute later, after some strained conversation in the cockpit, they declared an emergency and requested clearance to return to the airport. Although it was immediately granted, the Citation never made it. It slammed into the waves at about 243 knots, in a steep nose-down, left-wing-low attitude. All six people on board died instantly. Although privacy laws protected his identity, it's very possible the patient awaiting the vital organs was another fatality.

But what could have happened? The NTSB investigation into the crash laid the blame squarely on the flight crew, saying, "The National Transportation Safety Board determines that the probable cause of this accident was the pilots' mismanagement of an abnormal flight control situation through improper actions, including failing to control airspeed and to prioritize control of the airplane, and lack of crew coordination." It believed it was likely that copilot Hoyes had inadvertently engaged the autopilot instead of another control switch positioned next to it, which created difficulty in handling the aircraft. And then, instead of following emergency procedures, the pilots became confused, panicked and distracted. Of course, the NTSB's conclusion was based on probabilities. Because small jets of that type are not required to have a "black box" that records all flight data, investigators could only surmise based on the cockpit voice recordings and a knowledge of the flight characteristics and control locations on the aircraft. It seems strange that two experienced pilots would make such basic errors, but it wasn't the first flight that went down in Lake Michigan under mysterious circumstances. And sadly, it hasn't been the last.

THE LOST PLANES OF THE WOLVERINE AND THE SABLE

As World War II ramped up in Europe, it was obvious that the United States needed to develop and train fighter pilots who would be capable of flying from aircraft carriers sent to aid the war effort. However, training on the ocean presented some real dangers, as detailed by Taras Lyssenko, who is the cofounder of a company that works to recover the old warbirds for the National Naval Aviation Museum: "We were dealing with, on the East Coast, the German U-boats, and the Japanese actually had really good submarines on the West Coast. So if you were a young pilot having to learn to land on an aircraft carrier, well, it was hard enough doing that, let alone if the ship, the aircraft carrier was dodging torpedoes from submarines."

The navy soon realized that the perfect training ground was right under its noses; Lake Michigan had waves and winds that equaled or exceeded what would be found on the high seas, and with Chicago perched right on the shore, it would have nearly unlimited access to equipment, transportation and support. But first the service branch needed to get some aircraft carriers. In 1942, the Navy purchased the *Seeandbee*, a massive steam liner that belonged to the Cleveland and Buffalo Transit Company. After some modifications, including the addition of the landing deck, the ship was commissioned as the USS *Wolverine* and placed into service in August 1942. Shortly thereafter, a second, even larger passenger ship, the *Greater Buffalo*, entered service as the USS *Sable*.

Between 1942 and the end of the war, more than fifteen thousand pilots were trained on these ships, and not all were naval aviators. Several units of Army Air Corps pilots, including the legendary Tuskegee Airmen, also earned their wings over the lake. Of course, there were expected training accidents, but it seemed as though the toll was quite high. There were more than two hundred reported incidents, and at least 130 planes crashed and sank into Lake Michigan, killing eight pilots and about forty crewmen. By the end of the war, the waters off the coast of Chicago resembled an aircraft graveyard.

Since then, several groups have attempted to recover and restore these historic treasures. According to author and military historian Adam Loman, the wreckage includes planes such as the F6F Hellcat, P-39Q Airacobra, SBD-2P Dauntless, P-40F Warhawk, P-47D Thunderbolt, SB2U Vindicator and the FM/F4F Wildcat. About forty aircraft have been recovered so far and can be seen at aviation museums around the country, including the Air Zoo Flight Discovery Center in Kalamazoo, Michigan.

Most of these brave pilots and crewmen went on to battle in the waters of the Pacific Ocean, and some never returned home, offering the ultimate sacrifice for their country. However, there were several who never got the recognition, falling instead to the deceptively familiar waters of Lake Michigan.

THE AIR SHOW NO-SHOW

Traverse City, Michigan, bills itself as the Cherry Capital of the World, and it takes its festivals seriously. The National Cherry Festival is a yearly weeklong event that includes music, food, entertainment and a spectacular air show, which takes place over west Grand Traverse Bay. Visitors can relax at the Beer Tent and watch daredevil aerobatics by teams such as the U.S. Navy Blue Angels or grab some barbecue and wander among an amazing assortment of aircraft, ranging from home-built experimental models to classic warbirds and even some modern military jets.

On July 3, 1998, a two-seat Aero L-39 Albatross, being flown by a veteran pilot named Don Schaller, cruised over Lake Michigan, preparing to participate in the show. The Albatross is a high-performance single-engine jet developed in Czechoslovakia and used by many countries in eastern Europe as a military trainer. In the rear seat, Don Rodriguez, a flight instructor at Northwestern Michigan College, was along for the ride. Both men were excited; it was Schaller's first time participating in an airshow, and it was also his twenty-ninth wedding anniversary with his wife, Christine. Rodriguez and his wife, Patricia Delonnay, were planning on attending his fortieth high school reunion later that evening. There would be plenty of time to celebrate after the aircraft's scheduled fly-by.

Around 6:00 p.m., Schaller radioed that he was twenty-seven miles out and heading back to the airport. At that time, radar showed the jet in the vicinity of South Fox Island. Flight controllers asked him to call in when he was five miles out and said that they'd then give him instructions for entering the show pattern. Not long after, the controllers realized that the Albatross had vanished from radar, and they were unable to get a response from the pilot. Soon, Coast Guard helicopters began scouring the area, but they found nothing. It made no sense. Both pilots were extremely well qualified and had given no indication that anything was wrong. The aircraft was equipped with parachutes and ejection seats, although no one knew for certain if the seats were functional. The weather was clear and calm, and the Albatross was known to be a reliable and relatively simple plane to fly. What could possibly have gone wrong?

The next day, a Canadian C-130 cargo plane and the Blue Angels' C-130 "Fat Albert" joined the Coast Guard, and despite a painstaking search over many miles of land and water, not a single clue turned up to explain the fate of the Albatross. On July 9, a spokesman for the Michigan State Police grimly announced that the search was over: "We've exhausted every lead we have, every lead that's come in. We don't have any debris… we don't have any oil slicks. We're not closing our investigation and will continue to accept calls and tips, but we're suspending our search until we receive new information. We now believe the aircraft is located in the waters of northern Lake Michigan."

To date, the plane has yet to be found. All that is known is that it lies somewhere deep within the Lake Michigan Triangle.

THE FURY OF THE WAVES

Waves are not measured in feet or inches—they are measured in increments of fear.
—Buzzy Trent, U.S. pioneer of big wave surfing

For as long as men have ventured onto the water, ships have foundered and sent the brave—or sometimes foolhardy—mariners to a watery grave. Uncharted reefs, rogue waves and sudden tempestuous storms can maim even the sturdiest of vessels. Although many people envision these dangers as exclusive to the world's vast oceans, the inland seas of the Great Lakes are every bit as deadly as the wildest ocean. Lake Michigan, which is the second-largest of the Great Lakes by volume, is in fact one of the deadliest. There's no consensus on the number of shipwrecks beneath the deep, foreboding waters, but most agree there are probably up to ten thousand, especially if one includes early indigenous craft. Only about three hundred have been identified to date, and many others are now nothing more than a rotting pile of timber that leaves no hint of the life and livelihood they once represented.

The vast majority of these wrecks can be explained logically. For example, the Armistice Day Storm of 1940 was a uniquely severe weather event that brought hurricane-force winds and massive waves towering up to thirty feet. It wreaked tremendous death and devastation across the region. On Lake Michigan alone, three large freighters and numerous smaller vessels plunged to the bottom, taking the lives of sixty-six sailors. But what about those that can't be explained so easily? What about those that simply disappear beneath the waves, leaving little clue as to the forces that doomed them? Perhaps some of these are victims of the Lake Michigan Triangle.

THE UNLUCKY *ROSA BELLE*

The *Rosa Belle* (registry no. 21302) was a sturdy, two-masted schooner that was built in 1863 by the Leander H. Boole Shipyard in Milwaukee. Its wooden hull stretched 106 feet from bow to stern, with a gross tonnage of nearly 115 tons. The ship was one of the many hardworking sailing vessels designed to haul lumber and other cargo across the Great Lakes to quell the insatiable demands for building materials in the burgeoning cities that dotted the shorelines.

It seemed, however, that the sinister forces of Lake Michigan intended to doom the *Rosa Belle* from the start. Its first deadly encounter was in August 1865, when a sudden angry squall forced it ashore near Grand Haven, leaving the ship severely damaged. Although its crew was rescued, Captain Peterson was brutally pummeled with falling spars and rigging during the grounding, and he succumbed to severe head injuries shortly thereafter. The following year, the wreck was purchased by Squire & White from Grand Haven, eventually rebuilt and returned to lake service in April 1876. Thirty years and a few owners later, a strange, undocumented collision once again sent the *Rosa Belle* to the shipyard for rebuilding. This accident would be a foreboding warning of things to come. Twice it had faced the wrath of the lake, and twice it returned to its waters. How long would its luck hold out?

By 1919, after more than five and a half decades of challenging its fate, the *Rosa Belle* was sold once more. Its new owners were an Israelite sect that lived in a commune on High Island, part of the Beaver Island archipelago in northern Lake Michigan. The House of David was a millenarian group that believed the second coming of Christ was imminent, and its members prepared for this eventuality by following strict guidelines, which included taking a vow of celibacy, living a communal life, following an austere vegetarian diet and refusing to cut their hair or beards. They believed that, as chosen ones, they would enjoy a gift of one thousand years of life in heaven on earth. These beliefs seemed quite odd to the mostly staid and practical Michiganders, but in spite of general skepticism, the mainlanders eventually developed a healthy trade relationship with the strange cult. The Israelites revived an old deserted lumber mill on the island and planted a wide variety of crops. Whatever wasn't used to directly support the commune was sold for a handsome profit. And that's where the *Rosa Belle* fit into the plans.

Two of the most valuable commodities produced were potatoes and lumber, especially the much-coveted Birdseye maple, which brought the highest price from furniture factories in Grand Rapids and Ludington. Despite its age, the *Rosa Belle* was a capable workhorse, hauling loads of cargo to these and other various ports around the lake. It was typically piloted by Brother Ed Johnson, who often relied on his children to round out the crew. Some have questioned whether or not Johnson held a valid captain's license and noted that he often hired an experienced captain from outside the commune to ride along. However, when the ship prepared to set sail with a load of potatoes and maple lumber in October 1921, Johnson suddenly and strangely refused to make the trip. His son, Bert Johnson, later stated that his dad had an ominous "premonition" of disaster that so frightened him he insisted on remaining on shore. No amount of persuasion could convince the old sailor to board the ship. And so, on that fateful voyage, the *Rosa Belle* cast off with a new captain at the helm, an outsider named Erehart Gleise. The weather was calm and pleasant, except for an eerie lingering fog that hung low over the water. Its intended destination was Benton Harbor, near the southern edge of Lake Michigan. It never made it.

A few days after the *Rosa Belle* sailed away from High Island, the *Ann Arbor* Car Ferry no. 4 of the Grand Trunk Milwaukee Car Ferry Company reported spotting the overturned hull of a ship about fifteen miles east of Kenosha, Wisconsin. There was no sign of any crew, and from the visible damage to the stern, it appeared that there had been a collision, possibly with one of the large steel ore boats that traversed the lake. The ship's lifeboat was missing but was later found floating empty, along with several life belts. Rescuers assumed that the crew had been taken aboard the larger ship and would soon be returned safely to port. After all, except for the omnipresent and peculiar fog, there were no reasons that a capable sailor couldn't evacuate a sinking ship in calm, peaceful waters and strike out in the seaworthy dinghy. While they waited for a report of the collision, the steamer *Cumberland*, piloted by U.S. Marine captain Alexander, headed out to tow the wreck into Milwaukee. They located it about thirty miles from shore where it had drifted and began the arduous job of recovery. Lake Michigan, however, wasn't quite ready to give up its prey. Shortly after they attached the tow line, a sudden and vicious nor'easter swept down and churned up furious waves and wind, separating the line and forcing the *Cumberland* to make a run to safe harbor. It would be a few days before the steamer, accompanied by the

U.S. Coast Guard, was finally able to drag the *Rosa Belle* into Racine Harbor, where it was later beached for salvage.

It only got stranger from there. In the coming days, no other ships on the water reported a mishap involving another vessel, and no trace of the crew ever surfaced. After closer examination of the wreckage, the Coast Guard cryptically declared that the damage perhaps wasn't caused by a collision with another craft, but it offered no further explanation. It seemed as though the *Rosa Belle* had crashed into thin air! How could a sturdy ship be fatally wounded in calm seas if not by collision? There were no reefs or other underwater dangers in its path. And why hadn't its crew taken to the lifeboat? The U.S. revenue cutter *Tuscarora* promptly returned to the area to search for bodies, but none was ever recovered. Records of the fatalities are sketchy. Some sources claim that nine crew members were missing and presumed dead, while most others insist there were eleven aboard. A report from the House of David, however, mentioned a total of twenty-eight passengers and crew. No one seems to know how many souls were really lost on that fateful voyage.

The Israelites did not replace the schooner. Soon after the disaster, some of the brothers built a forty-foot power boat, which they christened the *High Island*. It was used primarily to pick up goods needed by the commune, which was facing dwindling membership and financial difficulties. In early 1923, Michigan authorities issued an arrest warrant for Benjamin Purnell, the sect's founder, accusing him of "debauchery of young women," a charge that stemmed from allegations that he maintained a harem of young virgins for his personal pleasure. Rumors swirled that the island was actually a penal colony with "bones scattered on the beach" and numerous unreported deaths of residents who were buried in unmarked graves. The State of Michigan, alarmed by reports of such depravity, filed suit to dissolve the Israelite House of David. By late 1927, the Israelites had deserted the island, leaving behind only a small handful of Ottawa Native Americans and itinerant farmers who remained until the Armistice Day blizzard of 1940 forced them to relocate to the relative safety of Beaver Island.

Today, the island is owned by the State of Michigan and managed by the Michigan Department of Natural Resources as part of the Beaver Islands State Wildlife Research Area. However, there is one final curious tale that surrounds its history. In the 1850s, James Jesse Strang—an American religious leader, politician and self-proclaimed monarch—established a "kingdom" on nearby Beaver Island for the Church of Jesus Christ of Latter-day Saints. Strang reportedly amassed quite a substantial "royal treasury," which he buried for safekeeping on High Island. In 1856, he fell victim to an assassin's bullet, leaving behind only the clue that the wealth was buried thirty paces from a large tree visible from the island's northeast harbor. However, shortly thereafter, logging on High Island began in earnest, and any potential landmarks that might have led to the treasure were destroyed. All this only adds to the mystery surrounding the final voyage of a ship that sailed into an eerie fog and never returned, as well as the enigmatic island it once called home.

The *W.C. Kimball* and a Voyage Interrupted

The *W.C. Kimball* (registry no. 81176) was a wooden two-masted schooner built in 1888 by M. Orms of Manitowoc, Wisconsin. Although it was a relatively small ship—just shy of sixty-four feet in length and weighing only forty tons—it was a dependable vessel for hauling small cargo loads across the lake. In the early 1890s, the *Kimball* was based out of Northport, Michigan, and spent most of its days running consignments of salt, roofing shingles and potatoes to ports along the Michigan coastline and down to Chicago. In May 1891, Captain James Stevens, sailors Charles Kehl and Karl Andreason and one lone passenger—a Mr. William P. Wolfe, who was described as a "Northport correspondent"—set sail along the usual route. That spring had been unusually hot with scant rain, leaving the parched landscape as dry as tinder. As a result, the Grand Traverse region was plagued by incessant wildfires that sent smoke and burning embers swirling across the shores and out over the lake. The acrid haze burned eyes and nostrils and greatly reduced visibility on the water.

It was under these conditions that the *Kimball* left Manistee Harbor on Wednesday, May 6, headed home to Northport. That Friday, as it sailed north of Frankfort near Point Betsie, a swift gale reportedly swept the north end of the lake, compounding the misery from the smoke and ash. It must have felt like sailing through the gates of Hell. It wasn't until a few days later, when the steamer *Lawrence* reported passing through a floating debris field of shingles, that anyone suspected disaster. It seemed clear that the *Kimball* had sunk in the gloomy depths, but why? The brief storm was surely not enough to sink the sturdy schooner. Immediately, the steamer *Williams of Charlevoix* was dispatched to look for survivors, but no trace of the ship or its crew was found. Other than the shingles, which had apparently floated free when it went under, the only signs that the *Kimball* was lost were discovered the following summer, when Charles Kehl's cap, Karl Andreason's trunk with letters inside and one small blue hatch cover washed up on the shore near Leland, Michigan. Some thought that it had collided with another vessel in the blinding smoke, but no other ships were reported damaged or missing. Others speculated that it had broken apart in the gale, but the ship was built to withstand such punishing waves and wind and the absence of wreckage belied that theory. With no obvious cause at hand, the *Kimball* became just another lost and unexplained casualty of the Lake Michigan Triangle.

That is, until September 2018, when shipwreck hunter Ross Richardson was demonstrating his side-scan sonar to his cousins while out for a casual family trip to North Manitou Island. Suddenly an interesting target came into view on the screen. Richardson immediately recognized it as some type of sailing vessel, and he knew that several had foundered in the area. Unfortunately, it sat more than three hundred feet below the surface, well beyond Richardson's ability to dive. Undeterred, he contacted technical diver Steve Wimer II of Milwaukee to aid in the identification. Initially, the team thought it had discovered the *Emily*, which sank during a fierce gale in 1857. However, a sharp-eyed friend noticed that pictures of the wreck showed iron ropes on the deck, which weren't used on the Great Lakes until after the Civil War, nearly a decade after the *Emily* had gone down. With the *Emily* ruled out, Richardson spent the long, cold winter months buried deep in intensive research. After poring over more than six thousand historical records, he had narrowed the possibilities to a handful of likely ships, including the *Kimball*. Luckily, early photographs of the schooner existed, and Richardson noticed a defining feature: the *Kimball* sported running lights, a rare addition for Great Lakes vessels of the time. If they found running lights, they could positively identify their wreck.

Once the balmy spring weather finally arrived, Richardson and Wimer set up a new dive, this time adding more crew and an ROV (remote-operated vehicle) capable of transmitting live images to the dive boat. While ROV pilot, Bryan Dort, guided the submersible, Wimer carried a video camera to record footage from every angle of the wreck. Soon they had their answer; the distinctive running lights—now completely encased in quagga mussels—were still visible in the frigid and deep waters. The *Kimball* had at last been found, nearly 130 years after it last roamed the lake. But instead of providing answers, the discovery only raised more questions.

To the divers' surprise, the ship appeared pristine and intact. It sits upright in the silt, its masts and rigging erect and undamaged as though it's ready to continue on its ghostly voyage at any moment. The hatches are still battened down, and a lifeboat, complete with oars, rests serenely on its stern. Wimer, after exploring the wreck, said in disbelief, "You could raise it, drain it, and sail away on it today." The ship seems to have been swallowed whole by the deep lake, without apparent cause or explanation. The upright masts and rigging wouldn't have withstood a rogue wave or devastating winds, and there are no signs of collision damage to the hull. And why didn't the crew take to the lifeboat if disaster loomed? It seems that the *Kimball* simply sailed into the frigid abyss as it dared to take on the deadly triangle.

THE MISSING CAPTAIN GEORGE R. DONNER

The last week of April 1937 had been a rough one for Captain Donner. His ship, the *O.S. McFarland*, had loaded up 9,800 tons of coal in Erie, Pennsylvania, bound for Port Washington, Wisconsin. Although the surrounding fields and forests were brimming with life at the onset of balmy spring weather, the upper Great Lakes still remained choked by late winter ice. Navigating safely through the treacherous floes took all the skill the fifty-eight-year-old skipper possessed, and after long, grueling hours at the helm, he was completely exhausted. Once the *McFarland* finally cleared the Straits of Mackinac and sailed into northern Lake Michigan on April 28, Donner decided to take a well-deserved rest. It was, ironically, his birthday, but there would be no thought of celebration until his cargo was delivered and his crew safely ashore.

After a quick final check of their position, he handed over command of the ship to his chief mate, leaving instructions to wake him as they neared their final destination. With that, he retired to his cabin for a long-awaited nap and gently closed the door. Despite his fatigue, he appeared to be in good spirits as the arduous journey neared its end. The remainder of the voyage was uneventful, and the *McFarland* made good time as it passed through the relatively calm and ice-free waters of Lake Michigan. Those waters, of course, were smack in the middle of the Lake Michigan Triangle.

About three hours later, as the ship neared Port Washington, the second mate headed to Donner's cabin to waken him as requested. He tapped softly, but there was no response. After a pause, he knocked more firmly and called out the captain's name, but only an eerie silence greeted him. Now rather concerned, he twisted the door handle firmly, only to realize that it was locked from the inside. Worried that Donner had fallen ill, the second mate immediately summoned other crew members, and together they forced their way into the cabin. To their surprise and dismay, it was empty. The neatly made bunk showed no signs of recent use, and there was no hint that the captain had been in there at all since he had reported to the helm much earlier that morning. His comb and razor sat precisely where he had left them on the small desk, awaiting the next morning's ablutions. What could have happened to Donner? The tiny portholes in the room were much too small for an adult to squeeze through, and in any case, the crew certainly had no indication that Donner was depressed or suicidal. But if he had left to grab a snack from the galley or perform an unexpected task, how could his door have been locked from the inside?

Panicked, they searched the entire ship from stern to bow, but the captain seemed to have vanished into the ether. It was highly unlikely that he had accidentally gone overboard—the waters were relatively calm, and the experienced skipper certainly wasn't prone to carelessness on deck—but they scanned the waters nonetheless. Despite the crew's heroic efforts, George Donner was gone. Once the *McFarland* docked safely in Port Washington, they quickly reported the frightening incident, and the authorities hurriedly began searching the deep, cold waters of the lake. No trace of his body was ever found, and to this day, the captain's disappearance—from a locked cabin, no less—is an unsolved mystery.

THE MAJESTIC *LE GRIFFON*

Lake Michigan has long served as a valuable trade route. As early as the 1600s, French explorers developed trade relationships with the various native tribes, exchanging European-made goods such as cloth, iron tools and cooking kettles for the rich bounty of furs possessed by the indigenous people. Although this fragile partnership was mutually beneficial in many ways, it also introduced misfortune in the form of guns, alcohol, deadly communicable diseases and slavery to the tribes. Both sides viewed the other with a healthy dose of uncertainty and apprehension, and occasionally tensions ran high.

Prior to the late 1600s, the typical boat used on the Great Lakes was the canoe. A canoe could be either made out of birch bark or a hollowed-out tree. Lake canoes were often large—sometimes up to thirty-five feet in length—but the primary method of propulsion was oars or poles. However, the renowned French explorer Robert de La Salle had other plans. La Salle owed a great deal of money to his creditors in Canada, and when he came to the region in the late 1670s, he knew that a simple canoe couldn't possibly hold all the riches he needed to settle his debts. Instead, in January 1679, he began construction on a magnificent new sailing vessel, which he christened *Le Griffon* after the mythological half-eagle, half-lion beast that is said to guard the gold and precious belongings of the kings. It was built primarily at the mouth of Cayuga Creek, near Niagara in western New York. Although a grueling winter, loss of their supply ship and rumors of a possible Indian uprising slowed construction, the craft was finally ready for its maiden voyage in August of that year, a tortuous journey through Lake Erie, Lake St. Clair and up through Lake Huron, before finally stopping at Mackinac Island.

Upon arrival near the Michigan shores, the crew was greeted by an enthusiastic group of Huron Indians, who turned out in birch-bark canoes by the hundreds to surround and examine the "giant canoe" that had sailed to their waters. The finished ship was indeed a remarkable sight: a massive forty-five-ton barque, fitted with three masts (although that number is in dispute—some sources say only one or two) and several square sails. Seven cannons flanked its rails, and a carved figure of its mythical namesake rode proudly on the bowsprit, warding off any potential enemies. It was the first full-sized sailing ship on the Great Lakes and has been considered the precursor to modern commercial navigation.

La Salle caught up with some deserters from his previous crew on the island but apparently, in turn, lost a few current crew members, who had had enough of the arduous expedition. He left his trusted lieutenant, Henri de Tonti, behind to deal with the personnel issues, with plans to rendezvous later, while he and the remaining crew sailed on to Washington Island at the head of Green Bay. There, a great number of Potawatomi tribesmen awaited him, including their revered head chief, Onanguissé. La Salle and Onanguissé had encountered each other several times previously, and they had a great deal of respect and affection for each other. By all accounts, the visit was a resounding success. The friendly Potawatomi had hunted more than twelve thousand pounds of fur, and La Salle had important and practical items such as fishhooks, guns, gunpowder, knives, kettles and other tools, as well as some fancy adornments such as beads and brightly colored coats, to offer in trade.

On September 18, 1679, *Le Griffon* sailed away from Washington Island, heavily laden with its valuable cargo. La Salle was quite pleased; it should be enough to satisfy his debts once he returned to Canada. He had decided to remain behind with a small crew and continue exploration along the

Lake Michigan coast. The plan was for the ship to pick up Tonti and the additional crew from Mackinac Island, head on to Niagara for supplies and then return for La Salle and the others so that they could continue their quest southward. The day of its departure, a Catholic priest named Father Hennepin, who was accompanying La Salle, noted that there was a "light and favorable wind." The crew ceremoniously fired a single cannon shot in farewell as it headed north from Washington Harbor. *Le Griffon* was never seen again.

There are plenty of theories regarding the ship's fate. Some claim that the vessel simply went down in a sudden fierce storm that hit the next day, which brought towering waves and high winds. Others blame the captain and crew with scuttling the ship and making off with the fortune in furs. Yet others blame Ottawa and Huron tribesmen, whom they claim murdered the crew and burned the boat. There's even a supernatural explanation: Metiomek, an Iroquois Indian prophet, believed that the giant ship was an affront to the Great Spirit, and he placed a solemn curse on it. When it failed to return, the Indians whispered that it had "sailed through a crack in the ice." *Le Griffon* was one of the earliest recorded victims of the Lake Michigan Triangle, and its true fate may never be known.

Over the years, various explorers have claimed to find the wreck, but only one group has provided any credible evidence: the Great Lakes Exploration Group, headed by a Charlevoix, Michigan couple named Steve and Kathie Libert, insist that they have located it off the Garden Peninsula in northern Lake Michigan. However, many archaeologists disagree, and the Liberts' claim has been a contentious one, involving a federal court battle with the State of Michigan that has lasted more than a decade as of this writing. In any case, there's still no explanation of what might have caused the sinking. Yet on foggy nights, some people have reported seeing the ghostly majestic ship cresting the waves near Washington Island. Perhaps Metiomek's curse did send the great ship through a mysterious crack in the ice, where it endlessly repeats its lost voyage?

THE *W.H. GILCHER* AND ITS UNLUCKY TWIN

The *W.H. Gilcher* was a lake steam freighter built in 1891 by the Cleveland Shipbuilding Company for partners Gilchrist, Gilcher & Schuck of Sandusky, Ohio. At 302 feet, the ship was nearly as long as a football field, and it was one of the first freighters to sport a steel hull, not the traditional iron or wood construction typical of Great Lakes steamers. Steel construction allowed the builders to design a larger ship capable of carrying greater loads, one that would withstand the frequent Great Lakes ice better than a wooden hull. With a capacity of 140,000 cubic feet of bulk cargo, the *Gilcher* and its sister ship, the *Western Reserve*, were looking to revolutionize Great Lakes shipping. Instead, their short lives were gripped by misfortune and tragedy.

The *Gilcher*'s first brush with trouble occurred in April 1892, less than a year after its maiden voyage. Its wheel chains parted, and it ran aground on the Canadian side of the St. Clair River. Three American tugs hurried to its rescue, but it took several laborious hours to finally free the ship. Less than one month later, the bad luck would continue. As it churned through the late-spring pack ice near Duluth, the ship's wheel broke, requiring a tow all the way to Buffalo for necessary repairs. It certainly wasn't an auspicious first year for the new freighter.

Then, in August 1892, news of disaster struck. The crew at Lifesaving Station No. 10 in Michigan's Upper Peninsula were roused when a bedraggled and exhausted sailor named Harry Stewart breathlessly stumbled up to their door. Stewart was a wheelman on the *Western Reserve*, the *Gilcher*'s twin, and the story he told was a heartbreaking one of terror and survival. While steaming in ballast through Lake Superior—just north of the Michigan Triangle—to pick up a load of ore in Michigan's iron range, the *Western Reserve* encountered a small gale. It wasn't much of a storm, certainly nothing that the crew hadn't faced dozens of times before. On board was owner Captain Peter Minch, who was an experienced and well-liked mariner; his wife, three children and his sister-in-law; and a crew of twenty-two. At about 9:00 a.m. on the morning on August 30, the vessel was riding the waves smoothly with no sign of trouble until, suddenly, a deafening crashing and groaning sound filled the air. Without warning, the ship began to tear apart right before their horrified eyes.

Stewart later recalled jumping over a growing three-foot chasm in the decking to reach a lifeboat as the ship split in two. The vessel carried two lifeboats: a wooden yawl and a metallic one. Captain Minch and his family, along with a few officers and crew, leaped into the wooden boat, and the rest of the crew piled into the metal craft. Within ten minutes, the *Western Reserve* sank out of sight, with its engines still roaring and propellers helplessly churning the water. The horror, however, had just begun. Moments later, the metal lifeboat capsized in the waves. The other boat immediately went to their aid, but they were successful in rescuing only two people. Still, the yawl was now dangerously overloaded and taking on water as they struck out for Whitefish Point, some sixty miles away. As day turned into night, a large steamer passed right by them, but they had no means of signaling for help. Stewart said they tried burning one of the ladies' shawls to draw attention, but it was too wet to light. Although they screamed and waved furiously, the other ship continued on, unaware of the tragedy taking place off its port side.

By morning, the yawl was approaching shore, but the danger hadn't abated. Violent waves kicked up along the shoals, and the tiny boat capsized, sending its already cold and exhausted passengers into the frigid water. Only Stewart, who was an expert swimmer, survived. He would forever be haunted by the screams of the women and children, followed by the deadly silence as the lake slowly claimed its victims. After nearly two hours of fighting the turbulent surf, he finally crawled ashore and fell unconscious on the deserted beach. When he awoke, he faced a twelve-mile hike through the wilderness to the safety of the lifesaving station. Upon hearing his story, the crew began an immediate search, but it was clear that it was a recovery mission only. Strangely, Captain Truedell at the station claimed to have had a wildly vivid dream of the disaster before it even occurred. The details were so shockingly clear that he immediately recognized the body of Captain Minch when it washed up on the shore a few days later.

News of the *Western Reserve*'s sinking stunned the maritime community, but most blamed the disaster on the crew's practice of filling only the forward ballast tanks when running empty of cargo. An unnamed authority at the time was quoted as saying, "If such was the case all doubts as to the cause of the accident are at rest, for according to calculations, the strain amidships under the circumstances would be almost beyond belief…no vessel could stand for any length of time the strain thus imposed when running into a head sea." But if the sinking of the *Western Reserve* foreshadowed disaster for the *Gilcher*, it appears that no one was paying attention.

Just two months later, in October 1892, the *Gilcher* departed from Buffalo with a crew of eighteen (some reports claim twenty or twenty-two), carrying 3,080 tons of coal bound for Milwaukee. On Friday, October 28, its captain, L.H. Weeks, reported its position as it passed through the Straits of Mackinaw. It was expected in Milwaukee the following day. On that fateful Friday, a fierce storm swept over the northern part of the lake. Many ships took shelter, but the *Gilcher*, along with others, continued to battle the waves. Later that evening, Captain Duncan Buchanan of the schooner *Seaman* encountered the ill-fated ship, which showed no signs of life: "We were about 20 miles northeast of North Manitou Island and 15 miles due west of Fox

Island light, at 8 o'clock, Friday night, when we sighted the *Gilcher* just ahead. She was in our track and we burned a torch for the steamer to make room for us. She made not a move and was lying with her head west-northwest, directly in the wind, and did not appear to be working her wheel more than to keep her head to the wind. We had to turn out and pass within 300 feet of her. No attention was paid to us."

By the following morning, other ships were reporting a large debris field off South Manitou Island that seemed to indicate the loss of a ship. Initially, other mariners suspected that the debris came from the schooner *Ostrich*, which was sighted bottom-up near the beach. As more wreckage came ashore, however, it was clear that the *Gilcher* had foundered as well. Some theorized that the two had collided, while others assumed that the ship had bottomed out on the nearby shallow reef. Yet others insisted that the steel used in building the ship, which was manufactured by the now obsolete Bessemer process, was impure and unable to withstand the strains placed on the structure. Interestingly, the lifeboat strongback was later recovered, which showed it had been struck by an axe, leading investigators to conclude that the crew might have attempted to slash through the canvas covers in a panic instead of removing the covers normally. But why did the ship appear deserted when the *Seaman* passed, although it showed no obvious signs of distress?

Few of the crew were ever recovered. Second mate Thomas Finley's wife even hired a psychic in a desperate but unsuccessful attempt to give her husband a proper burial. In January, the newspaper *Leelanau Enterprise* reported, "Mrs. Thomas Finley accompanied by Mrs. M.J. Zinysfer, a clairvoyant, doctress, and life reader of Buffalo, were in town today on their way to North Manitou Island. Mrs. Finley has strong hopes of recovering her husband's body."

Although many theories abound, we might never know why the new and state-of-the art twin freighters slipped helplessly beneath the waves. To date, neither ship has been recovered. As of this writing, the *W.H. Gilcher* is the largest unidentified shipwreck on Lake Michigan…and one of the best-known victims of the Lake Michigan Triangle.

MARY MCLANE AND AN UNLIKELY STORM

Not all encounters in the Lake Michigan Triangle result in death and destruction. Some are simply strange and unexplained, like the experience of one hapless tugboat crew. The *Mary McLane* was a small harbor tug that worked the lake coastline, helping ships through the Chicago Harbor and in and out of the Chicago River. It was one of a dozen steam tugboats owned in part by William Harmon, and it had a tow capacity of about twenty tons.

July 12, 1883, dawned a beautiful, clear and sunny summer day in Chicago. Bright blue skies and gentle waves graced the horizon, although the temperature was unseasonably chilly. Visibility was nearly unlimited, with no sign of foul weather to come. At about 6:00 p.m., the *Mary McLane* was about twenty-five miles north of the city doing routine chores when the crew was surprised to hear the ominous rumbling of thunder. They peered at the sky in confusion, since the sun still shone brightly and there was not a cloud in sight. Suddenly, chunks of ice began to rain down from above. At first, they were amused by what seemed to be an impossible clear-sky hailstorm, but that soon turned to alarm as the chunks grew larger. Within moments, huge bricks of ice slammed furiously onto the deck, forcing the crew to dive to safety to avoid the lethal deluge. One deckhand narrowly escaped injury as a massive wedge barely missed striking his head. The onslaught continued for nearly half an hour, leaving prominent dents in the wooden deck. Then, as quickly as it began, it stopped.

As the men peeked warily from the safety of the cabin, they realized that no one would believe their unlikely story, so one mate quickly plucked a large block of ice from the deck and stored it in the galley's icebox. When they returned to dock, they were met with skepticism at first. There had been absolutely no sign of any foul weather on shore, and indeed, the cloudless blue sky still stretched to the horizon. But soon, to the crew's relief, another tug captain who had been nearby the *McLane* arrived and confirmed the bizarre event. No one could offer any explanation for the strange weather anomaly, but the incident did make newspapers across the country. And the little tugboat's dented and scarred deck held testament to the mysterious things that could happen if one dared venture out into the mercurial lake.

THE MYSTERY OF THE *THOMAS HUME*

The *Thomas Hume* was a sturdy three-masted wooden schooner that plied the waters of Lake Michigan in the busy lumber trade of the late 1800s. It was roughly 132 feet long with a 26-foot beam, and it was well designed to withstand the punishing waves of the Great Lakes. That much is certain, but the ship's origins are nearly as murky as its eventual disappearance. Current sources state that it was built in 1870 in Manitowac by Joseph Hanson and was originally christened the *H.C. Albrecht* after its first owner, Captain Harry C. Albrecht. However, newspapers of the time list the ship as the "*H.C. Albright*," built in 1880 by Jasper Hanson for Captain Harry C. Albright. Most likely, the old newspapers are correct.

In any case, the *Albright*—or *Albrecht*, if you prefer—was eventually sold to lumber tycoons James McGordon and Charles Hackley of Muskegon, Michigan. Hackley and McGordon owned one of the largest mills in the area, forested their own timberland and had a fleet of schooners at the ready to ferry the sawn lumber to Chicago in support of its massive housing growth. In 1879, the partners moved their new ship into dry dock for repairs and upgrading. No expense was spared as they replaced the decking, strengthened the framing and added the third mast. The refitting enabled the ship to carry about 250,000 board feet of lumber each trip, about enough to build eighty standard-sized houses. Unfortunately, McGordon wouldn't live to see the renovated schooner back on the water; he died unexpectedly in 1880. Shortly thereafter, Hackley offered a partnership to his trusted bookkeeper, a young Irishman by the name of Thomas Hume. Finally, in 1883, now seaworthy and rechristened in honor of the new partner, the *Thomas Hume* began a regular schedule of hauling lumber from Muskegon to Chicago.

On May 21, 1891, the ship unloaded its cargo at the Chicago docks and prepared to return to Muskegon. The skipper was Harry Albright, who happened to be the son of its original owner and former namesake, and he was known as someone who wasn't deterred by a little rough weather. (Current sources typically list the captain as Harry Albrightson, but several original newspaper accounts state that the schooner was piloted by "Capt. Harry C. Albright's son," who lived in Chicago; it's easy to see how the name was inadvertently changed over the years.) The day was chilly and damp, with a storm brewing across the lake, but that didn't dissuade the *Hume* and another Hackley and Hume ship, the *Rouse Simmons*, from setting out together to begin the trek back home, although the *Hume* was one crewmember short on its final voyage. Saxe Larson, an experienced sailor and regular member of the crew, was supposed to be onboard but had a change of heart—or perhaps a premonition—at the last moment and didn't show up in time for the departure. After leaving Chicago and heading east into the wind and waves, both captains were frustrated by the slow progress they were making as they labored in the heavy seas. Eventually, the *Rouse Simmons* decided to return to port for the night and set sail when the weather was more favorable. The *Hume*, however, continued on. That would be the last time it was seen.

When the skipper of the *Rouse Simmons* finally reached Muskegon late the following day, he wasn't terribly surprised to find that the *Hume* hadn't yet arrived. He figured that Captain Albright had finally grown tired of fighting the wheel and had settled into port somewhere along the route and would show up in due time. Perhaps he'd even tolerate some good-natured ribbing about surrendering to the vagaries of the lake. As the hours turned into days, however, the sickening realization began to dawn that something had gone horribly wrong. Soon, rumors began to fly.

Hackley and Hume, the vessel's owners, were convinced that the schooner had been run over and left to sink by a large freighter. Partner Thomas Hume was quoted as saying, "We don't mind the loss of the boat very much, but don't like losing the seven men on board her." After sending out telegrams to all possible ports, pleading for information, the company posted a $300 reward for any information on the sinking. They guaranteed anonymity, hoping that the reward might entice a seaman to come forward and implicate a guilty captain. Experienced lake sailors mostly dismissed the idea. Dozens of vessels traversed the area daily, and the tug *Sill* methodically scoured the lower lake in search of signs of the *Hume*, yet not a stick of debris was ever found. Surely the ship couldn't endure a deadly collision and sink without a single trace? Others blamed the captain, saying that he was "in the habit of crowding up too much canvas"—carrying too much sail for the conditions—which might make the schooner unwieldy. That theory, however, still wouldn't explain the lack of debris. It seemed that the ship had simply vanished into the ether.

In June, Jules Verne, the marine editor of the *Chicago Times*, advanced a new theory that was heavy on conspiracy. He was certain that the *Hume* had been spirited away to an obscure port, repainted and given the same name as another schooner that ran the Muskegon-to-Chicago route. He based this on the fact that the vessel in question moved rapidly between the two ports. Thus, he reasoned, it was probable that actually two ships were working as a team while pretending to be a single hardworking craft and crew. He never explained how this alleged trickery would benefit the ship's owner or what possible purpose it would serve, and his theory was widely scorned.

Just when it seemed that things couldn't get any stranger, a bottle washed up on the shores of Benton Harbor three months after the sinking. The note inside read, "We the undersigned are the passengers of the *Thomas Hume*. The schooner's hold is rapidly filling with water and we have no hope of escape. We are on the St. Joseph course and been drifting for hours. We have friends in McCook, Neb. and Elkhart, Ind. Please notify them of our fate." It was signed by Mr. Wilbur Grover and Mr. Frank Maynard. Almost immediately, the schooner's owners pronounced it a hoax. They insisted that the ship carried no passengers, and it normally sailed a more northerly route. And if it had indeed taken on water, it carried a perfectly serviceable yawl that the crew would have used to escape. In addition, typical wave patterns on the lake made it unlikely that the bottle could have floated as far north as Benton Harbor. It appeared to be merely a cruel prank, and the fate of the *Hume* remained a mystery.

That is, until 2006, when diver Taras Lyssenko of A&T Recovery was searching for old naval aircraft in southern Lake Michigan. He was working on behalf of the National Museum of Naval Aviation, and his team had already identified more than thirty World War II planes in the area. A new sonar hit looked promising, but instead of an aircraft, they discovered a century-old wooden schooner in nearly perfect condition. Lyssenko turned the wreck over to a group of Chicago-based professional divers and the Michigan Shipwreck Research Associates, who began the arduous task of identifying it. Although they found no clear-cut proof, the evidence that they had discovered the *Hume* was overwhelming; the size, general location and artifacts all pointed to the lost schooner. However, nothing they found explained why the ship went down. There was no damage suggesting a collision, and it still didn't make sense why the well-built ship would have sunk, or why the crew wouldn't have taken to the lifeboat. And what about the cryptic message in a bottle? As it turns out, there's some evidence that it might not have been a prank after all. The still, icy-cold fresh water of the lake had preserved the ship and its contents quite well. Divers found fancy designer clothes and fine shoes that seemed an unlikely wardrobe for hardworking lake sailors. And, as stated in the note, the wreck was positioned along the St. Joseph route and not the more northerly course toward Muskegon. It seems that we will never know for certain how many souls fell victim to the relentless waters—or why.

THE *J.H. HARTZELL* AND THE LADY TIED TO THE MAST

Sometimes the unspeakable horrors that face us are not caused by something supernatural, but rather by the fears and frailties of our fellow humans when they are confronted with life-or-death choices. Such was the fate of Lydia Dale.

Lydia was a hardworking and sturdy woman with a kindly nature and a talent for the culinary arts. For many years, she was employed by S.W. Flowers, a Toledo merchant, as a cook and housekeeper. Eventually, she moved on to Buffalo, New York, where she was later hired as a cook aboard the *J.H. Hartzell*, a 130-foot wooden cargo schooner that carried ore from the iron ranges of Michigan's Upper Peninsula to smelters and factories around the Great Lakes. The *Hartzell* was built in 1863 by shipbuilder H.J. Williams of Buffalo, and it'd already had some bad luck on the lakes. In April 1868, the schooner mysteriously caught fire while in dry dock in Detroit, leaving it and several other nearby ships severely damaged. After being towed to Toledo, it was rebuilt at Bailey's shipyard and returned to service.

On Monday, October 11, 1880, the *Hartzell* sailed from port at L'Anse in Lake Superior, at the base of the Keweenaw Peninsula. It was loaded with 495 tons of iron ore bound for the Frankfort Furnace Company, located in its namesake town on the eastern Lake Michigan coast. The five-day trip through the lakes was uneventful. The weather remained pleasant and calm with favorable wind, and Lydia kept the crew well fed. When the ship reached its destination several hours before sunrise on October 16, Captain William A. Jones signaled that he would wait until daylight to enter the harbor so that he could more safely navigate through the many nearby sandbars that might trap his heavily laden ship. The crew dropped anchor and settled down for a few hours' rest. That rest, however, would be short-lived.

Around 6:00 a.m., well before the autumn sun would begin to streak orange across the sky, the winds shifted suddenly to the southwest and began to blow in earnest. Soon, a wintry mix of rain, snow, hail and sleet started pounding the decks as the waves grew in intensity. In what seemed like barely a heartbeat, the *Hartzell* found itself trapped in the tempest of a full-blown gale. Unable to raise the anchors in the violent waves, Captain Jones ordered the crew to release them so that he could safely turn head into the wind, but it was too late. A giant wave tossed the ship bow-first into a sandbar, where it sank into what would soon become its grave. Although it was only about three hundred feet from shore and in just a little more than a dozen feet of water, the roaring wind and ravaging waves began to tear the ship apart. As hatches ripped away and the hull began to fill with water, the crew huddled on deck in the fierce maelstrom of ice and turbulence, praying for rescue. Lydia, who had been down in the galley doing meal prep, was terribly sickened and disoriented by the bucking and lurching of the trapped vessel and required the assistance of four sailors to help heave her stout body above deck, where she cowered among the others. As daylight dawned and the drama played out offshore, a young boy, the son of a local fisherman, spotted the floundering ship and ran for help.

Almost immediately, a large crowd began to gather on the sandy bluffs towering above the water. Although the town of Frankfort had a lifesaving service, it was manned by volunteers and had virtually no equipment that would be of any use to reach the stranded sailors during such a frightful storm. While a messenger raced on horseback to the well-equipped Point Betsie Life-Saving Station some ten miles distant, the locals used burning logs to spell out "LIFEBOAT COMING" on the face of the bluff to offer some hope and comfort to the *Hartzell*'s terrified crew. Others frantically tore away brush and small trees to clear a path for the rescuers.

At that time, the most commonly used piece of lifesaving equipment was the Lyle gun, a small cannon-like device that used a black powder charge to shoot a rescue line up to seven hundred yards offshore. It could be directed at swimmers floundering in the surf or, as in this case, shot to a struggling ship and secured to create a lifeline between ship and shore. Passengers could then be safely evacuated through the use of a breeches buoy—basically a life ring with a canvas sling in the center that allowed a person to step into it like they were putting on "breeches"—or they could climb into a "surf car," a metallic cigar-shaped contraption that was watertight and capable of carrying more than one person at a time. The buoy or the surf car would then be pulled to safety by the rescuers on shore. Although surprisingly effective, the equipment was heavy and unwieldy. Although the Point Betsie crew had leaped into action the moment the messenger arrived, it would take some precious time to load and drag the gear the ten miles to the Frankfort shore and move it into position. According to the U.S. Life-Saving Service's description of the scene, "Even with the impediments removed, so precipitous was the activity that it took the unified effort of 27 brawny men, by actual count, and a span of stout horses, to gain the summit, only about 20 feet being made at a time."

Eventually, with the Lyle gun in place, a surfman was able to hit the ship on just the second try, and the line was secured. After twenty harrowing minutes in blinding sleet, and with more than two dozen men pulling in unison, the ship's first mate was brought on shore in the breeches buoy. He was almost incoherent from hypothermia, but he managed to say that a woman was on board the ship, and she was very ill. The rescuers quickly decided to switch to the surf car, and with an even greater sense of urgency, they ran it over the line to the ship. When they hauled it back and opened the hatch, they were shocked to see two crewmen huddled inside and no sign of the ill woman. The men said that the woman would come on the next attempt. Once again, the rescuers raced to send the car skimming across the waves and struggled mightily to haul it safely ashore. Upon return, it contained the captain and second mate. The lifesaving crew and volunteers were furious now; it was unthinkable that any man of the sea—any gentleman of any sort—would save himself before a helpless woman. They barked at the captain for an explanation, and he said defensively, "She's as good as dead anyway, but they'll send her the next trip." The sun was setting and the rescuers were exhausted, but they knew they had to make one final effort to save the poor woman. For the last time, they sent the surf car careening through the gathering darkness. When it reached the beach, out crawled the final two crewmen. The crowd exploded, demanding answers. The men were nervous and evasive, but they claimed that Lydia was dead and that they had left her frozen body lashed to the rigging. It was now fully dark, the ship invisible in the dim and stormy gloom. There was nothing more that could be done until daylight.

The next morning, as dawn breached the sky, those on shore were horrified to see that the masts and rigging of the ship—along with Lydia's body—had disappeared into the surf during the night. "It is, and doubtless will always be, an open question: in what condition the hapless woman was left upon that mast," stated the Life-Saving Service report. Sadly, that question would soon be answered. Seventeen days later, Lydia's decomposing body washed ashore. After careful examination, the coroner reported that her death had been caused by drowning. She had indeed been alive when she was abandoned in the ship's rigging by the crew. And although an inquest was called, the crew of the *Hartzell* had all disappeared rather than face public scorn for their spineless treachery. They hadn't actually committed a crime, but there was widespread anger and disgust at their selfish actions. Upon hearing of her demise, however, her former employer, S.W. Flowers, requested that her body be sent to Toledo, where he would pay all expenses to give her a proper funeral and burial. Although she was callously disregarded in her final hours, at least her life would be celebrated after her passing.

In the end, this was a story of kindness and cruelty, of heroism and cowardice. A story of another victim who fell prey to the dangers of the Lake Michigan Triangle.

The Wreck of the *Andaste*

The *Andaste* was a slope-sided steel-hulled freighter built by the Cleveland Shipbuilding Company in 1892. It was an odd-looking ship with a design similar to a whaleback, but with the latest triple expansion steam engine, the *Andaste* was a powerful workhorse capable of carrying nearly three thousand tons of sand, gravel or crushed stone. Although it was originally built to haul iron ore from Lake Superior to the lower Great Lakes, the growing necessity for building roads and highways across the country soon led to an explosion in demand for concrete and paving materials. In 1925, the ship was refitted with a self-unloading crane and other gear that made it an attractive carrier, especially for ports that couldn't previously be serviced by a bulk freighter. It was then chartered to the Construction Materials Company of Chicago, where it made regular runs ferrying aggregate from the massive gravel pits near Grand Haven, Michigan, to meet the insatiable needs of Chicago's exploding growth.

On Monday, September 9, 1929, the *Andaste* was docked at Ferrysburg, Michigan, on the Grand River, where it took on a load of two thousand tons of aggregate. It was a routine trip that its captain, Albert L. Anderson, made four times a week. According to Coast Guard records, at 9:03 p.m., he piloted it through the Grand Haven harbor piers and headed out into the lake. Anderson had been sailing the Great Lakes for more than forty-eight years and was looking forward to retirement at the end of the shipping season. Soon he could relax and spend more time with his wife and family. Instead, they would be planning his funeral.

About an hour into the journey, the wind began to blow with a howling fury. The weather service had issued gale warnings, but the *Andaste* carried no radio equipment and wouldn't receive the notice. Other ships scurried to ports, but the freighter lumbered on into winds that reached sixty miles per hour. When it didn't arrive in Chicago as expected the following morning, the search began. Initially, an extensive air and water search turned up no sign of the missing ship, but a few days later, the fishing tug *Bertha G* reported that it had found a vast field of debris, apparently from the *Andaste*. Originally it was believed that there were twenty-seven men on board according to the ship's roster, but for reasons unknown, two crewmen had been left behind; those men later helped identify pieces of the wreckage. One, helmsman Joe Collins, was so relieved at escaping his close brush with death that he drank himself into a stupor and was arrested in Grand Haven for public intoxication. He was fined twenty-five dollars but claimed that he couldn't pay because his wallet and all his belongings were on board the ship. If perhaps he stayed back because he had a premonition of disaster, he wasn't the only one.

Mrs. Pauline Whitaker, the mother of quartermaster Harold J. Whitaker, claimed that she had known for weeks that her son wouldn't return. Shortly after his last visit with her, a clock in the home had suddenly stopped working, and her son's picture flew off the wall. She was certain that these were omens foreshadowing his death. Harold had previously been employed on the steamship *Theodore Roosevelt*, and this had been his first—and last—assignment on the *Andaste*. Another member of the crew, a fourteen-year-old schoolboy named Earl Zitlow, was on his very first voyage. He had begged his parents for a year to allow him to sail the lakes, and they had finally grudgingly relented. He was last seen peeling potatoes in the galley as the vessel prepared to leave port. And for one family, the loss was doubled. Mrs. Kibbey, a mother with five young children, lost both her husband, Claude Kibbey, and her father, Jim Bayless, each of whom served as engineers on the freighter. Apparently, both men had eerily expressed reservations before the trip. A family member, Mrs. Goodwin, who had spoken to Claude Kibbey shortly before he set out, said he seemed reluctant to return to the *Andaste*: "I don't know whether he had a premonition of trouble or not, but he seemed to sense something. He said he was sure if anything ever happened on the lake, that he'd be all right as long as the engines held out." However, his father-in-law didn't seem to share his optimism. "Claude," said Jim Bayless, "if that boat ever springs a leak, we'll all go."

On September 17, searchers retrieved a section of board that was later identified as part of the woodwork of the captain's cabin. On it, Anderson had scrawled, "Worst storm I have ever been in. Can't stay up much longer. Hope to God we're saved." Sadly, the *Andaste* had no such salvation. Over the next few days, bodies of the doomed seamen began to wash ashore. Eventually, sixteen bodies—eleven of whom were wearing life jackets or preservers—were recovered. The remaining nine were presumed to have been trapped below decks and forever entombed in the cold Lake Michigan water. In a chilling twist, one young sailor's body washed up on the shore next to his family's farm near Grand Haven, arms frozen and outstretched as if he was struggling to reach out to his loved ones with his final breath.

No one knows why the *Andaste* went down, and the wreck has not yet been found. It had certainly faced tough storms before. Had it been overtaken by a rogue wave? Torn asunder by the gale? Did its cargo shift and cause it to roll? Right now, it is just known as one of the many victims of Lake Michigan's deadly forces.

For weeks after the sinking, the ship's loyal mascot, an Airedale named Queenie, worriedly paced the dock at Ferrysburg, her eyes searching the waters for the return of her beloved crew. Although she rarely joined them on the boat, she was always waiting, tail wagging, to greet them upon arrival. This time, her wait would be in vain.

THE DISAPPEARANCE OF THE CHRISTMAS TREE SHIP

The *Rouse Simmons* was a wooden three-masted schooner built in 1868 by Allen, McClelland & Company of Milwaukee. It went through several owners in its forty-four years on the lake, including a stint with Hackley and Hume, who owned it at the time of sinking of their other ship, the *Thomas Hume*. Eventually, it was purchased by a group including Captain Herman Schuenemann for use in a wildly successful family endeavor: the yearly delivery of thousands of evergreen "Christmas trees" from the northern forests to the eager crowds in Chicago. Because the schooner had been built especially for the lumber trade, it was a perfect vessel for the job. Schuenemann would fill every inch of the ship with trees, sometimes stacking them so high on deck that the ship barely rode above the water. Once docked in Chicago, he and his crew would string up electric lights and gaily decorate a few trees to create a festive display for the throngs who would flock to the Water Street dockage to bring home a little Christmas cheer. His wife, Barbara, and daughters Hazel, Pearl and Elsie used some of the branches to fashion wreaths and garlands, which were snapped up as quickly as they could be made. The annual arrival was a beloved part of the holiday season for Chicagoans, and it's little wonder that the ship was affectionately known as the "Christmas Tree Ship." Schuenemann was generous, often donating trees to churches and orphanages, which gained him the nickname "Captain Santa." Sadly, Herman's elder brother, August Schuenemann, had died while sailing a load of Christmas trees to Chicago aboard the schooner *S. Thal* in 1898. However, the family tradition lived on, and it was a yearly lucrative venture that kept the bill collectors satisfied.

On November 17, 1912, the ship sailed from Manistique, Michigan, with a reported crew of sixteen. However, it's not clear how many people were actually aboard the schooner. The kindly captain had offered a free ride to several lumberjacks so that they could join their families back in Chicago for the holidays. But when it left Michigan, it was at least one crewmember short: Hogan Hoganson had a last-minute change of heart about sailing that day. "It was the rats that gave me my first hunch that trouble was ahead," he said. "The rats had deserted the ship while we lay in Chicago harbor, and all the way across the lake as we sailed for our cargo, the old saying had been ringing in my ears: 'the rats always desert a sinking ship.'" In Manistique, Hoganson was part of the crew that loaded the cargo, and he grew increasingly concerned about the massive load of trees that filled the hold and was stacked on every available surface on deck, taller than the tallest sailor. With no lifeboats aboard and impossibly heavy cargo, Hoganson abruptly decided to quit. The captain warned him that he wouldn't be paid if he didn't complete the trip, but the fearful and superstitious crewmember was undeterred: "I had some money and so I took a train for Chicago. Here I am—and the others?" Some accounts claim that several members of the crew deserted, but many of the stories seem to have been embellished to capitalize on the drama.

Apparently, Hoganson wasn't the only one with a forewarning of disaster. Captain Nelson, who was a partner of Schuenemann's in Chicago, had also seen the rats streaming out of the ship as it prepared to leave for Manistique. He mentioned it to Captain George Demar of the Chicago Harbor police, saying that he feared it was a bad omen. What caused the rats to leave? Is it possible they had an instinct that trouble lay ahead? The weather on the route from Chicago to Manistique was clear and pleasant—"Just like midsummer," according to Hoganson—so there should have been little concern as the ship sailed empty to pick up the cargo. It was only on the return voyage that tragedy would strike.

What happened next has been the subject of dispute for more than one hundred years. Historic reports claim that it was caught in a terrible snowstorm and struggled to make shelter in Baileys Harbor, Wisconsin, before it was blown back out into the lake. The next sighting was reported by the lifesaving station in Kewaunee on November 23, where a surfman spotted the ship flying its flags at half-mast, a sailor's signal for distress. The station had a gas tugboat, but it was already somewhere out on the lake, so they couldn't render aid. Instead, they contacted the next lifesaving station south at Two Rivers, which immediately dispatched a motorboat to search for the stricken ship. The station crew searched until darkness but apparently never found a trace of the schooner, although some legends claim that the surfmen caught a quick glimpse through driving snow of the ice-laden ship riding low in the water before it slipped away forever. However, modern-day researchers have raised questions about those dramatic accounts.

To begin, it wasn't lost in a blinding snowstorm with zero visibility. Although a violent blizzard did strike later that day, it didn't hit until well after the *Rouse Simmons* would have gone down; the visibility around the time it was lost was reported as six miles, although the wind and waves were strong and building. Secondly, when the wreck was discovered in October 1971, it was found in 170 feet of water about six miles off Point Beach. When researchers reconstructed the search area of the Two Rivers crew, they concluded that the rescue boat was never farther than a few miles from where the ship sank; had it still been afloat, the crew most definitely would have seen it. Divers have since brought up several artifacts from the wreck, including an electric lightbulb that must have been intended for decoration in Chicago, since the ship itself had no electricity. They were amazed to discover that the bulb still lit up when tested, after nearly sixty years underwater.

So, why did the *Rouse Simmons* sink with all hands lost? A few weeks after the foundering, a bottle washed ashore with a note inside that was signed by Captain Schuenemann. It read, "Friday…everybody goodbye. I guess we are all through. During the night the small boat washed overboard. Leaking bad. Invald and Steve lost too. God help us." Based on the position of the wreck when it was found, it appears that the crew was trying to anchor into the wind, but the depth of the water and fierceness of the waves made it impossible. Some theorize that a rogue wave washed over its bow and dragged it to the bottom. Others think that freezing waves across its deck turned to ice and that the accumulated weight was too much to bear. Careful examination of the wreck hasn't answered the mystery with any certainty.

After the tragedy, Schuenemann's eldest daughter, Elsie, publicly proclaimed that she did not need or want any charity and that she would pay off all of her father's debts—about $5,000 from the loss of the ship and cargo—through her own hard work. The December 11, 1912 *Inter Ocean* quoted her as saying, "I can pay that, every dollar….I'm alright, I can fight my way out some way. But the families of sailors and timber cutters on the boat may be really in need. Please look them up….I understand that some need money badly." She and her mother and sisters subsequently continued the tree business, using another three-masted schooner named the *Oneda*, which closely resembled its sunken predecessor, until they eventually switched to moving the cargo by train in 1920. The cherished Christmas tradition thus lived on, although the reason that the Christmas Tree Ship and Captain Santa were lost to the deep cold lake might never be known.

THE TRAGEDY OF THE *CARL D. BRADLEY*

The funeral procession stretched nearly two miles, as almost every able-bodied resident of the small port town of Rogers City, Michigan, population less than four thousand, marched in solemn grief to the memorial service. The lake freighter known as the "Queen of the Lakes," the *Carl D. Bradley*, had gone down in a late season gale on November 18, 1958. Of the thirty-five crew on board, thirty-three had perished and twenty-three of them were from Rogers City. Nearly every person in the town had experienced the loss of a friend, a neighbor, a husband or a family member, and fifty-three children were left without fathers.

But how could the well-built and modern freighter have foundered? The ship had just passed a U.S. Coast Guard safety inspection two weeks before. At 639 feet, the *Bradley* was the largest self-unloading ship of its time and the flagship of the Bradley Transportation Company. It would be another twenty-two years before another ship was launched that rivaled its size. It was also the only fully electric ship in the Bradley Transportation fleet, with a generator that powered everything from its huge fixed-pitch propeller to the massive refrigeration units in its galley. Most of its career was spent hauling limestone from a large quarry near Rogers City to various deep-water ports on Lake Michigan, but due to its size and steel construction, the *Bradley* also served as an ice-breaker in early winter and late spring months at the Straits of Mackinac, clearing the way for smaller ships to navigate.

On November 17, it unloaded a cargo of crushed stone at Gary, Indiana, in what was supposed to be its final trip of the season and then headed northwest in ballast toward Manitowoc, Wisconsin, to be put in dry dock for the winter. Before it got very far, however, the company ordered it back to the Port of Calcite at Rogers City to pick up one more load of limestone for a rush order. Most of the crewmen were unhappy, as this meant that they might miss Thanksgiving with their families. The captain, fifty-two-year-old Roland Bryan, hoped that the trip would be quick and uneventful and reassured the grumbling sailors that they'd be home on time. He was wrong.

Captain Bryan was an experienced seaman who prided himself on delivering his cargo on time, but he wasn't careless. As they headed back toward Rogers City in gusting wind and building waves, he decided to pilot his ship to the west, close along the Wisconsin coast, to avoid the worst of the weather. It was only when he reached the Cana Island Lighthouse on Wisconsin's Door Peninsula that he steered east toward Michigan. By that time, the winds had increased to sixty-five miles per hour with heavy seas, but the *Bradley* was riding the waves smoothly with no sign of trouble. At 5:30 p.m., First Mate Elmer Fleming routinely radioed to Port Calcite to tell them they'd arrive around 2:00 a.m. No sooner had the message been sent than the crew was startled by a loud *boom* that shuddered through the entire ship. At first, no one was certain what had happened, but they soon gasped in horror when they saw that the entire stern section of the boat was sagging in the water. Immediately, Captain Bryan realized that the unthinkable had happened: the *Bradley* had split in half. He sounded the general alarm and commanded the crew to put on lifejackets and abandon ship. As they scrambled for the lifeboats, Bryan was able to send one more message: "Mayday, Mayday! We are in rough seas; we have broken in two and are sinking." At that, the transmission abruptly cut out.

The desperate call for help was picked up by the U.S. Coast Guard, nearby ships and several commercial stations. A German cargo freighter, the *Christian Sartori*, was only about three miles away and immediately changed course to come to the aid of the doomed vessel, but as they watched through binoculars, they saw the lights of the *Bradley* flicker out. Moments later, the sky lit up with towering orange and red flames as the ship's boilers exploded. It was clear that the freighter had gone down, but they held out hope that some crew had reached the lifeboats. They had no way of knowing that the lifeboats had not been launched—only two were on board the ship, and both tangled in cables, preventing the crew from escaping into them. Only a small life raft floated free, which just four sailors were able to reach. Unfortunately, due to the fierce winds and waves, it took the *Sartori* more than an hour to reach the site, and when it did, its crew found nothing but debris and no sign of survivors. Exhausted and now fearing for their own safety, the would-be rescuers headed for the safety of Washington Island. What they didn't know is that there were indeed four survivors in the dark, brutal storm who were desperately clinging to a life raft and praying for rescue.

The U.S. Coast Guard cutters *Sundew* from Charlevoix, Michigan, and *Hollyhock* from Sturgeon Bay, Wisconsin, headed to the scene, but it would be many long hours before either arrived. Shortly after dawn the next morning, the *Sundew* spotted the ice-encrusted raft bobbing in the waves with four bodies aboard. Crewman Dennis Meredith was already dead from exposure, and Gary Strzelecki was barely clinging to life. He died after being transferred to the cutter. Amazingly, First Mate Elmer Fleming and watchman Frank Mays were both still alive, although covered in ice and severely hypothermic. They were carefully swaddled in blankets and given warm liquids, but they steadfastly refused to be taken to safety, insisting instead that the rescuers continue searching for any other possible survivors. Unfortunately, there were no more. Instead, the ships spent the remainder of their time recovering bodies. In all, sixteen bodies and the two survivors were recovered, with fifteen men never found.

What caused the massive ship to break in two? It was discovered that it had twice run aground in 1958, and neither incident had been reported. Was it possible that hairline cracks or metal fatigue doomed the great freighter? Or was it simply the fate of a ship that dared to challenge the deadly lake?

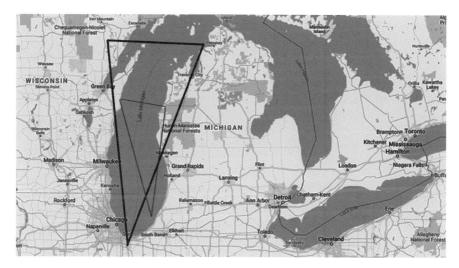

Although the original concept of the Lake Michigan Triangle only covered the area from Manitowoc, Wisconsin, to Ludington, Michigan, and south to Benton Harbor, strange and mysterious incidents are happening in and around the entire lake.

Northwest Flight 2501, a Douglas DC-4 prop liner like the one pictured, disappeared over Lake Michigan on a stormy night in 1950.

A cockpit view of a Boeing 727 like United Flight 389, which inexplicably flew into the water near Chicago in 1965.

An image of the three-point altimeter design that the pilots of United Flight 389 might have misread. Displayed here is an altitude reading of 10,180 feet.

A photo of the actual Beechcraft V35 Bonanza taken before it went missing west of Frankfort, Michigan. The pilot's body has never been found. © *Mark Pasqualina, August 25, 2013.*

An Army Air Forces C-54A Skymaster. Hundreds of these planes were converted to civilian use after the end of World War II.

The USS *Wolverine* docking in Chicago. The former steam-powered luxury cruise liner was purchased by the military and converted to an aircraft carrier. It spent World War II in the waters of Lake Michigan, where it trained pilots for air combat.

The Grumman F4F-3 Wildcat was an American-made carrier-based fighter aircraft that was used in the Pacific theater during World War II. At least thirty-seven of these were lost in Lake Michigan during training exercises.

A TDN-1 naval assault drone taking off from the deck of the USS *Sable*. These drones were part of a secret program during World War II to develop unmanned attack aircraft, and they could be radio-controlled up to a distance of eight miles. All three assigned to the carrier crashed into Lake Michigan.

TDN-1 drones were designed to carry a payload of bombs. In this training photo, the drone attempts to drop inert bombs on a towed target but missed. The aircraft flying near it is a Grumman Duck, a single-engine amphibious biplane, which was controlling the drone.

The *Rosabelle* was a wooden two-masted schooner that was found floating empty and damaged in Lake Michigan. Its crew was never found, and investigators couldn't determine what had caused the damage.

Cloud formation over Washington Island. Explorer Robert de La Salle's majestic sailing vessel *Le Griffon*—then the largest ship on inland waters—sailed from this harbor and was never seen again.

The *W.C. Kimball* was a wooden two-masted schooner that disappeared in 1891. In 2018, it was discovered upright and in pristine condition, three hundred feet below the surface, with no obvious reason for its sinking.

The *Andaste* was a steel freighter that broke up and sank in a storm. Some of the crew had premonitions of danger before its final voyage. *Wikimedia Commons.*

VISITORS FROM THE UNKNOWN

I can never look now at the Milky Way without wondering from which of those banked clouds of stars the emissaries are coming.
—*Arthur C. Clarke, author*

D o you believe in UFOs? If so, you're not alone. According to a variety of recent polls, roughly two-thirds of Americans believe that life exists elsewhere in the universe, and about 50 percent believe it's visiting us. While it's true that the vast majority of sightings can be explained away as misidentified aircraft or natural phenomena, there's a disturbing number of incidents that can't be so easily dismissed. Project Blue Book, the U.S. Air Force's study of unidentified flying objects, operated from 1952 until 1969 and investigated more than 12,600 sightings. About 22 percent remained unexplained, even after intense scrutiny. But Project Blue Book wasn't the first—or the last—U.S. government program designed to study the possibility of extraterrestrial activity on Earth. And we're not the only country attempting to answer the question. Across the globe, governments are watching the skies and wondering if we are being visited, and what those visitors ultimately might want.

Of course, when the subject of UFO encounters is raised, most people immediately think of Roswell, New Mexico, where in 1947, a purported crash of a flying saucer scattered strange debris for nearly a mile, as well as, some people insist, a number of alien bodies. The air force claimed that it was actually a crashed nuclear test surveillance balloon from the highly classified Project Mogul and said that the "alien bodies" were test dummies dropped from high altitude. What really happened is still being argued to this day. However, you don't need to head to the desert Southwest to see evidence of extraterrestrial visitors. The Great Lakes, and Lake Michigan in particular, are a hotspot for UFO sightings. On a side note, the more modern preferred term is "UAP," for unexplained aerial phenomena. You might also hear "USO," which stands for unidentified submerged object, since some of these visitors seem to have the ability to move with equal ease through water or air. This book will use the terms UFO/UAP interchangeably. But whether you believe the witnesses, or the sometimes feeble attempts to explain away what was seen, some of these events might make you gaze up at the skies—or into the watery depths—with a bit more wonder.

ARRIVAL AT O'HARE'S GATE C-17

It seems like the stereotypical UFO sighting is distant odd lights in a nighttime sky and a blurry dot, moving strangely across the heavens. But in this case, the large saucer-shaped object appeared in broad daylight, hovering silently just below the clouds, directly over a terminal at one of the world's busiest airports. The witnesses were all commercial pilots and other airport personnel who had seen nearly every manner of earthly flying machines during their careers. This wasn't one of them.

Tuesday, November 7, 2006, was a typical late autumn day in Chicago. Cool, with temperatures in the fifties and a low overcast sky that hung glumly over the city, reminding everyone that winter wasn't far away. At around 4:15 p.m., a United Airlines ramp employee was pushing back Flight 446, a Boeing 737 headed from Chicago to Charlotte, North Carolina, when he looked up and spotted a dark-gray metallic craft floating overhead. Stunned, he contacted the flight crew onboard the 737 and told them what he saw loitering over their jet. The pilot popped open a windscreen and craned his neck to look where the worker was pointing, and he saw it too. Soon other reports came in. A mechanic who was taxiing a plane to a nearby maintenance hangar stared in disbelief. Other pilots waiting nearby watched in amazement. As news spread quickly over internal radio channels, several United employees, including an airport manager, ran outside to take a look. Although accounts of the diameter varied—guesses ranged from six feet to twenty-four feet, as there was nothing nearby to help judge scale—all the witnesses agreed that it was dark gray, completely silent and like nothing they had ever seen before. It was clearly silhouetted below the cloud base, which was reported to be 1,900 feet that afternoon, and remained for about five minutes while a small crowd gathered to watch. Suddenly, with an instantaneous burst of speed, it punched upward through the clouds, leaving a small patch of blue sky visible where it had disappeared.

Official audio from the day captures some of the confusion. A United controller named Sue radioed a colleague, "Did you see a flying disk out by [Gate] C-17? That's what the pilot and the ramp guys are telling us at C-17. They saw some flying disc above them." The other controller clearly wanted no part of the incident and apparently feared for his reputation. He laughingly replied, "You guys been celebrating the holidays early over there or what? You having a Christmas party today? I have not seen anything, Sue, and if I did, I wouldn't admit to it. No, I have not seen any flying disc at Gate C-17. Unless you've got a new aircraft you're bringing out today that we don't know about."

The witnesses who saw it, however, weren't happy about being treated as if they were crazy and were only too happy to speak with the media. The United mechanic who was taxiing nearby said, "I tend to be scientific by nature, and I don't understand why aliens would hover over a busy airport. But I know that what I saw and what a lot of other people saw stood out very clearly, and it definitely was not an [Earth] aircraft." The United manager stressed that no matter what it was that people were seeing, any unidentified object in the immediate airspace could pose a real threat to the safety of air traffic. "I stood outside in the gate area not knowing what to think, just trying to figure out what it was," he said. "I knew no one would make a false call like that. But if somebody was bouncing a weather balloon or something else over O'Hare, we had to stop it because it was in very close proximity to our flight operations."

Despite the number of very reliable witnesses and the potential danger, authorities treated it as a joke or flat out denied that it ever happened. O'Hare controller and union official Craig Burzych noted with amusement, "To fly 7 million light years to O'Hare and then have to turn around and go home because your gate was occupied is simply unacceptable." And initially, both the FAA and United claimed that nothing had happened and that they had no record of any such incident. "There's nothing in the duty manager log…there's no record of anything," claimed a spokesperson for the airline. However, several employees later spoke of being interviewed by company officials, where they were warned not to ever speak of the event. The FAA, after repeatedly insisting that it had no information, suddenly backtracked after a reporter for the *Chicago Tribune* filed an official Freedom of Information Act (FOIA) request. It was then that the various audio recordings began to surface.

Almost immediately thereafter, an FAA representative claimed that it hadn't investigated because it was merely a rare meteorological event known as a fallstreak, or "hole punch cloud." These anomalies can happen when an aircraft passes through supercooled water droplets in a cloud, which turn to ice crystals and fall away, leaving a roughly circular hole in the haze. But there are a few problems with this explanation. Fallstreaks can only occur in freezing temperatures, and it was much warmer in Chicago that day. Also, the witnesses insisted that what they saw was clearly a distinct, solid object well below the overcast base, one that accelerated at unbelievable speed and disappeared. It was most certainly not simply an oddly shaped cloud. And they weren't the only ones who saw it that day. A man coming home from work in the suburb of Aurora, which is roughly thirty miles southwest of O'Hare, reported seeing a similar object earlier that day hovering between two clouds before it suddenly shot out of sight.

So why would authorities discount what could have been a serious threat to the safety of passengers and personnel? Another rationalization they offered was that the object wasn't captured on radar, so it must not have existed. Some experts disagreed, saying that radar technology cannot always capture hovering objects or those moving at extraordinarily high speeds. John Callahan, a former division chief of accidents and investigations for the FAA, said that there have been previous documented incidences where radar failed to pick up an object or provided contradictory or intermittent data. But most likely, it all boils down to the fact that the FAA is loath to acknowledge the possible existence of UFOs and refuses to accept the responsibility for investigating. The Aeronautical Information Manual (AIM), which is the FAA's official guide to basic flight information and air traffic control procedures, states that "persons wanting to report UFO/ Unexplained Phenomena activity" should contact an organization such as the National UFO Reporting Center (NUFORC). If "concern is expressed that life or property might be endangered," the manual says, "report the activity to the local law-enforcement department."

This attitude is anathema to many in the aviation community, who insist that we can no longer ignore these occurrences. "We must be proactive before an aircraft goes down. There have been documented cases where safety appears to have been implicated, and more and more we are coming to the point of view that we are dealing with an intelligent phenomenon," said Richard Haines, a former NASA space program scientist and science director at the National Aviation Reporting Center on Anomalous Phenomena (NARCAP).

Whatever it was that visited O'Hare Airport on that busy Tuesday afternoon, it was just one of the many unexplained objects that lurk in the skies above and around Lake Michigan. Despite our reliance on modern technology, this visitor appeared to arrive and depart without detection in one of the busiest airspaces in the world.

EAGLE RIVER PANCAKE BREAKFAST

Not all UAP sightings are observed by multiple people. Sometimes it's a highly individual experience that might leave the rest of us scratching our heads. That's the case in a 1961 report that came from Eagle River, a small Wisconsin town roughly 110 miles west of the Lake Michigan shores. Joe Simonton, a sixty-year-old chicken farmer and part-time plumber, was a well-liked and respected member of the community. He even dressed up as Santa Claus each year for the local chamber of commerce festivities. When he heard odd noises in his backyard one morning, however, he knew that it wasn't eight tiny reindeer. When Joe went out to investigate, he was more than a bit surprised to encounter a shiny, silver, saucer-like object floating above his yard. He estimated it was about twelve feet in height and thirty feet in diameter. As he watched, a hatch popped open and three short humanoids dressed in form-fitting black-and-blue spacesuits stepped out. They were wearing some sort of helmet, so he couldn't see their faces clearly, only that they had dark skin and dark eyes. One of the aliens held out a silver jug, and Joe somehow understood that they needed water. Ever the neighborly type, Joe went to his pump, filled the container and handed it back to his visitors. In return, they offered him a handful of something that they appeared to be cooking on a griddle-like device. It looked like some very thin, slightly burnt, holey pancakes.

Not wanting to appear rude, Joe took a bite of the still-hot food, but he later told a reporter that it was awful and "tasted like cardboard." With a wave of thanks, they climbed back into their ship and promptly departed. Shortly thereafter, dozens of reporters and thousands of curiosity seekers descended on his farm to see the "space pancakes" and gawk at the landscape. Even Project Blue Book and the air force took notice and launched an investigation, which it later closed and labeled as "unexplained." Lab analysis showed that the flat dry cakes were made of flour, sugar and grease, all items with a decidedly earthly origin. However, investigators concluded that despite what sounded like an outrageous tale, Joe honestly believed that it had happened exactly as he described. They theorized that maybe he had some sort of strange waking dream.

For his part, Simonton was embarrassed and upset that he wasn't taken seriously. He glumly remarked to a reporter that "if it happened again, I don't think I'd tell anybody about it." But as it turns out, Joe wasn't completely alone in his visions that day. Some of his neighbors reported seeing the strange craft earlier approaching the Simonton farm, and one even called the authorities to report the sighting. Only Joe, however, had the close encounter of the culinary kind.

WHAT THE COAST GUARD SAW

Two Rivers is a small, friendly Wisconsin city situated just south of the Door Peninsula on Lake Michigan's western shore. It proudly proclaims that it is the birthplace of the ice cream sundae, an assertion that is hotly contested by Ithaca, New York. As the story goes, in 1881, Ed Berner, the owner and namesake of Berners' Soda Fountain in Two Rivers, received a request from an adventurous customer who wanted some of the chocolate sauce from the soda fountain to be drizzled on his dish of ice cream. Ed charged him a nickel for the concoction. The customer was pleased, and Ed decided to begin offering it as a Sunday special in his restaurant. Soon the treat caught on, and Berner ordered some special canoe-shaped glass bowls to serve it in. In a modest attempt at marketing hype, Ed changed the spelling to "sundae" and began selling it every day of the week.

Nearly one hundred years later, the city would gain notoriety for something far less prosaic than sweet desserts. On July 23, 1978, just before 4:00 a.m., the U.S. Coast Guard Station (CGS) at Two Rivers received a call from its counterparts in Ludington, Michigan, who asked them to be on the lookout for a strange cigar-shaped craft that was moving across Lake Michigan and headed directly west toward Two Rivers. Ludington personnel had the object in sight and said that it displayed flashing red, white, orange and green lights and was moving at a calculated speed of more than 1,200 miles per hour. Shortly thereafter, Two Rivers CGS also saw it and called their colleagues to the north at Sturgeon Bay to advise them to keep watch as well. At 4:00 a.m., another call came in, this time from the St. Joseph CGS, nearly 300 miles to the southeast. A married couple had reported a cylindrical object with flashing white and colored lights hovering silently for nearly thirty minutes near Rocky Gap County Park, before it suddenly disappeared in a burst of speed. Although the object was moving incredibly fast, the frequency and distance between sightings seems to indicate the possibility of more than one craft. Observers noted that the white light was blindingly bright, and it strobed erratically across the water.

For the next several hours, the object zig-zagged wildly around the lake as Coast Guard staff from all four stations kept it under observation. It was also spotted by the crew at the Green Bay Lighthouse, and hours later, a similar craft was sighted as far north as the Apostle Islands in Lake Superior, nearly 250 miles to the northwest. During the event, crewmen from both the Ludington and Two Rivers stations snapped numerous 35mm photos and mailed them to the Commander of the Ninth Coast Guard District in Cleveland, Ohio. When UFO researchers later filed a FOIA request to review the images, they were told that the negatives had been "lost in the mail" and were never received. However, after a second request was filed, the story changed; now they claimed that one of the crewmen who had taken the photos had sold them to the *National Enquirer* instead of forwarding them to headquarters as promised. The *Enquirer* staff was apparently kind enough to share two color prints with the Coast Guard, but the story seemingly ended there. Frustrated researchers claimed that it was just another example of a government coverup. However, the dozens of CGS personnel and civilians who spent the early morning hours that July day watching the stupefying spectacle over Lake Michigan will never forget what they saw.

1994's WESTERN MICHIGAN "CHRISTMAS TREE" LIGHTS

March 8, 1994, was a cloudy, chilly and windy late winter day along Michigan's western coast. The temperature never rose above freezing, and residents likely yearned for the arrival of spring. Instead, the bright flashing multicolored lights in the late evening sky were much more reminiscent of Christmastime. The reports first began to roll in at about 9:30 p.m., when Joey Graves of Holland, Michigan, called to his parents to come look out the window at the strange lights he had seen hovering over a nearby barn. Soon the Holland Police Department was flooded with calls from concerned citizens, and it sent Officer Jeff Velthouse out to investigate. After borrowing some binoculars, he also saw what he later described as "five to six objects, some cylindrical with blue, red, white and green lights." By that time, hundreds of reports of sightings had been tallied among various authorities all along the Lake Michigan coast, stretching nearly two hundred miles from Ludington all the way south to the Indiana border. As Velthouse interviewed multiple witnesses in the Holland area, the 911 dispatcher for Ottawa County reached out to the National Weather Service (NWS) for a possible explanation.

The single employee on duty that night at the Muskegon NWS office was meteorologist Jack Bushong, who, up until that phone call, had been having a pleasant and routine shift. He was unprepared for what he'd hear next. After the dispatcher explained what was happening, Officer Velthouse took over the call, and the subsequent conversation—which was recorded—reveals some bizarre information. Bushong asked Velthouse, "What is really going on down there?" The officer explained, "We've had about 60 UFO calls....We've had reports from South Holland and over in northern Allegan County. Lots of lights moving all over the place."

Bushong sighed audibly and responded, "Oh jeez," before switching his radar to the manual mode and beginning a sweep of the area. "You could pretty much use it like a spotlight. I had two cranks to bring it up or down, or side to side," he explained in a later interview. It didn't take long to get a target on the screen. At first, what he witnessed was a single large blob, moving along at only about one hundred miles per hour, until it stopped and began hovering. Suddenly, it shot straight up into the air as he struggled to follow its path. "I'm getting it now at about 12,000 feet, it's a pretty strong return," exclaimed Bushong. "Oh my God, what is this? Now I'm getting three of them and uh, [they're] about separated by about 5,000 feet in height." Velthouse confirmed that matched exactly what he was seeing with his own eyes.

As the two continued their telephone conversation, the movement of the lights became more and more erratic. First, they formed a vertical triangle and then slowly rotated in unison to the horizontal. Just as quickly, they would zip away, before speeding back to re-form. "There were three and sometimes four blips, and they weren't planes," said Bushong. "Planes show as pinpoints on the scope, these were the size of half a thumbnail. They were from 5 to 12,000 feet at times, moving all over the place. Three were moving toward Chicago. I never saw anything like it before, not even when I'm doing severe weather." Occasionally, the targets skyrocketed as high as sixty thousand feet, which quickly discounted any thoughts that the radar might be picking up false signals from ground clutter effect. He continued tracking the objects on radar for more than two hours, sometimes seeing more than a dozen small blips moving rapidly between larger targets.

Eventually, Bushong reached out to the FAA control tower at the Muskegon County Airport to ask if it had observed anything unusual. An air traffic controller there confirmed that he had observed three unknown "aircraft" in a triangle formation off in the distance over Lake Michigan, but they weren't transmitting any transponder code and thus couldn't be identified.

Although the sightings of that night garnered worldwide news coverage, the National Weather Service immediately began walking back its involvement and downplaying its radar tracking. Bushong was instructed not to speak with the media, and an NWS spokesperson told reporters, "There is no relation between the UFOs and the radar tracks…we do not know what was causing these echoes." It wasn't until many years later that Bushong, then retired from the NWS, finally spoke freely. After relaying his story, he told the interviewer, "NWS didn't want to become the UFO reporting center for the United States, so that's really why they really had to duck and cover for this one."

USOs Under Lake Michigan?

With two major international airports and several smaller regional fields in the metropolitan area, Chicagoans are pretty used to seeing all manner of aircraft flashing overhead. That, plus the cacophony of tall buildings and bright lights everywhere, means that most residents don't take much notice of the skies overhead. However, every now and then, an unusual formation or strange movement catches the attention of those on the ground, and another UFO story hits the news. Such was the case in early 2021, when an observer captured a somewhat blurry video of seven glowing orbs moving slowly across the Lake Michigan skyline. According to the witness, the lights would hover, disappear and then sometimes reappear before fading away completely. The video quickly went viral, creating a firestorm of controversy online.

Opponents claimed that the video merely showed a string of normal earthly aircraft—aka commercial jets—lined up for approach to Chicago's Midway or O'Hare Airports. UFO enthusiasts insisted that the clip was anything but normal and said that the lights displayed characteristics unlike conventional craft. It wasn't long before yet another theory emerged. A UFO hunter named Scott Waring, who has an immensely popular YouTube channel, analyzed the video and said that although there were indeed commercial aircraft visible, other unidentified lights were moving in and out of the frames. To him, that could only indicate one thing: "The lights were so close to the water that sometimes the reflection of the UFOs could be seen. Aircraft can be seen flying over the lights once in a while, but the lights and aircraft stay far apart. These lights are a sign that there is an alien base below Lake Michigan. Absolutely amazing and even the eyewitnesses noticed other people not looking at the UFOs. Very strange how people are too busy to look out the window. 100 percent proof that alien base sites are at the bottom of Lake Michigan off Chicago coast."

Although it's hard to imagine extraterrestrial space ports under Lake Michigan, unidentified submerged objects have been captured on film before. The most famous was the encounter that some U.S. Navy pilots had while flying a routine training mission from the aircraft carrier USS *Nimitz* off the Southern California coast in 2004. When asked to check out and engage some strange radar contacts in the area, the pilots noticed an unusual churning of the ocean surface when, suddenly, a smooth white craft that resembled a giant Tic Tac breath mint emerged from the waves at unbelievably high speed and seemed to engage in a cat-and-mouse game with the fighters. It had no visible control surfaces or method of propulsion and seemed equally at home under water and in the air. The video, which was taken from the F/A-18Fs in pursuit, was eventually leaked to the public and later authenticated by the navy. USO encounters have since been reported across the globe, including some unverified sightings in the Great Lakes.

Of course, these tales are just a handful of the hundreds of UFO/UAP/USO sightings reported each year in the skies around Lake Michigan. Private agencies such as the National UFO Reporting Center and MUFON, the Mutual UFO Network, track and investigate reports, and the sheer number of calls they receive is mind-boggling. The U.S. government continues to conduct its own intelligence gathering, most recently under the Airborne Object Identification and Management Synchronization Group (AOIMSG), one of several government initiatives subsequent to the demise of Project Blue Book in 1969. After all, it's pretty disconcerting to think that there's an advanced civilization zooming around our planet that we can't always see, don't understand and can't control.

So, are there secret alien bases in the Lake Michigan Triangle, and could they be the cause of some of the strange happenings? It sounds far-fetched, but maybe it wouldn't hurt to look out the window once in a while, as Waring suggests.

STRANGE CREATURES
STALKING THE SHORELINE

There are very few monsters who warrant the fear we have of them.
—Andre Gide, French author and
winner of the Nobel Prize in literature

Cryptids are animals or beings that are thought to exist, even though there's no scientific proof of their existence. Most people have heard of famous cryptids such as the Loch Ness monster or Bigfoot, but there are dozens if not hundreds more that occur in local lore around the world. Some are rooted entirely in ancient legends and superstitions, while others are more recent manifestations described through eyewitness encounters. And yes, the shores of Lake Michigan are home to several of these beasts, lurking in the shadows and occasionally revealing themselves—either by design or accident—to unsuspecting trespassers in their territory.

CHICAGO'S MOTHMAN

Mothman first appeared far away from Lake Michigan, in the sleepy Appalachian town of Point Pleasant, West Virginia. On the night of November 15, 1966, two young couples, Roger and Linda Scarberry and Steve and Mary Mallette, were driving down State Route 62 near the

McClintic Wildlife Station. The area was previously home to the West Virginia Ordnance Works, which manufactured 500,000 pounds of TNT per day during World War II. Once the war ended, the plant closed, leaving behind eight thousand acres of heavily polluted land and ponds and dozens of igloo-shaped storage bunkers. Nature soon reclaimed much of the landscape, except for the igloos and an abandoned power plant building. At this time, it was a nature preserve, although locals still called it "the TNT area."

Roger was driving, and they all chatted happily as they cruised along. Suddenly, on the side of the road, they spotted a massive humanoid creature, which appeared to be about seven feet tall, with leathery wings that stretched to ten feet. Most striking, however, were the creature's huge eyes, which glowed blood red when struck by the headlight's glare. Terrified, Roger hit the gas and tried to speed away, but the creature leaped into the air and began to fly after the car. As the passengers watched in horror, it kept pace, even as they careened down the road at speeds in excess of one hundred miles per hour. They raced to the town's police station and breathlessly tried to describe the encounter. Although it was a crazy story, they were credible witnesses and hadn't been drinking; they had obviously seen something that badly frightened them. By 3:00 a.m., several local policemen and sheriff's deputies had descended on the TNT area to search for clues. Although there was no sign of the winged monster, they did hear strange noises and saw a cloud of dust rise up from behind one structure. There were also some odd footprints that they couldn't identify as coming from local wildlife. Soon, other sightings began to roll in, and the creature was dubbed "the Mothman" based on its vaguely insect-like appearance. Seeing Mothman was said to fill the observer with a deep sense of dread and anxiety. Reports continued for several months, most often around the TNT area, where people believed it lived, but he was also spotted in town near the Silver Bridge, a 1,760-foot-long span that crossed the Ohio River and joined West Virginia and Ohio.

At 5:00 p.m. on December 15, 1967, the bridge was packed with cars as townsfolk rushed about doing their pre-Christmas errands. Suddenly a strange groaning sound filled the air, and the Silver Bridge immediately collapsed into the river below, carrying with it thirty-two vehicles and forty-six victims, including two whose bodies were never found. As the town grieved the tragedy, the Mothman sightings abruptly ended, leaving some to believe that the creature had been a harbinger of doom, sent to warn Point Pleasant of the impending disaster.

For several decades, Mothman mostly disappeared from West Virginia and seemed to be moving north, with random and sporadic appearances reported in Indiana, Illinois, Wisconsin and Michigan. That is, until 2011, when he resurfaced with a vengeance in Chicago. The frequent sightings, which peaked in 2017 but have continued unabated to the current day, seem to primarily cluster around O'Hare Airport and the Lake Michigan waterfront. He certainly gets around. Like his counterpart in West Virginia, Chicago's Mothman tends to fill spectators with a deep dread and sense of foreboding, rather than the unbridled fear one would expect. Is it one singular creature, or does Lake Michigan host a den of cryptids that whirl through the city during the dark of night?

Chicago paranormal investigators—including groups such as MUFON, the UFO Clearinghouse, Phantoms & Monsters and the Singular Fortean Society—have interviewed witnesses and created a database of hundreds of Mothman encounters. Here are just a few of the stories:

April 7, 2017, at a public park near the lakefront:

I saw a large man, probably 7 feet or taller standing on the ground. It was solid black, but what really stood out were the large, and I do mean large, pair of wings that were folded behind him....I could not see its face as it had its face turned away from me and probably didn't notice me at first. It finally turned and noticed me and I saw the bright, ruby red eyes that appeared to glow from within....I felt like this thing could see right through me, read me, it knew what I was thinking, like it could stare right into my very soul. It was the most terrified I have ever been in my life. This thing stared at me for about 15 seconds, which felt like an eternity and then in a loud whoosh it unfurled its wings and screeched really loud, and jetted into the air.

June 29, 2017, in a Chicago neighborhood (police officer):

We were flagged down by a group of people who were pointing up to the top of an apartment building that was on the corner. [There was]...a large creature with wings on top of the building. We shined flashlights on it and it flew away. People crowded around said they had seen the creature flying over the neighborhood the previous two nights. We initially were doubtful about filing a report because we thought we would be made fun of for seeing Little Green Men. We finally filed a report as we did not want to violate protocol.

July 27, 2017, Chicago Loop (near lakefront):

I was leaving work at about 8:45 p.m. on Thursday night in the Loop. As I walked the two blocks to the nearest train station to go home, I saw a large bat-like creature that was perched on top of one the streetlight poles across the street from the Harold Washington Library. This creature stood about 7 ft tall and was sitting there motionless. This creature had a pair of glowing red eyes that appear to be fixated on something across the street. It stood there for about 6 seconds. That's when I saw a flash from a group of kids on the sidewalk as someone was taking a picture of this thing. It then spread open a large pair of wings, flapped them a couple of times and took off into the air. The girls from that group of kids screamed and they all took off running. I saw as it shot up and over the library and was gone in the matter of about two seconds.

August 21, 2017, on the lakefront and during an eclipse:

We were watching and observing as the moon began its transit when we heard a very loud scream. This sounded like squeaky truck brakes that squeal when you're pressing hard on them. At first, we thought that's what it was…maybe a CTA bus or big truck with brakes that needed changing or maintenance. We heard it again, this time it lasted about 3 seconds, whereas the previous sound was brief. I looked up to see a large object flying low over the docks that stick out in to Burnham Harbor from across the water.…This object looked like a large black bat, but also had humanoid features such as pronounced arms and legs.

August 8, 2019, at O'Hare Airport (from a commercial pilot):

I was taking the airport shuttle toward the terminal. As I looked out the window, I saw a large human with enormous wings and glowing red eyes perched upon a rail and looking straight at me. The being appeared to be squatting down on the rail but had its wings completely open and moved them slowly as he stared at the shuttle bus as we drove by. I knew it was watching me as its head swiveled and followed the shuttle as we passed. Its eyes locked on me the entire time. I was startled and I'll admit it, very frightened. Not only by this encounter, but the absolute boldness of this thing as it did not move or attempt to hide itself as we approached knowing that it could be clearly seen. We passed it on the outside lane and were at our closest approximately 15 feet away from where it was perched. It never once flinched or attempted to hide itself. It just stayed put and watched as we passed. When we passed, I attempted to look back and see if it was still perched there. I saw nothing and can only assume that it must have flown off when we passed.

February 21, 2020, at O'Hare Airport (from a security guard):

I rolled up to the fence and what I saw wasn't human; it looked like a very tall human, but it was solid black with glowing red eyes and it had a pair of wings that were outstretched that must have measured at least ten feet from tip to tip. I got out of my car and shined my flashlight at it, this thing screeched out loud, it almost sounded like the brakes on a train, loud and very high pitched. It then turned its back to me and flew straight up into the sky and took off like a bullet. I could see it as it took off, its wings flapping until it faded into the night. I heard it screech again and before I knew it, it was gone and I could not see it anymore. I drove back to where the truck was and I told the people there at the dock, and they said that people had seen it at least a few times.

May 21, 2020, at O'Hare Airport (from a commercial pilot):

As we're taxiing off the active runway and toward the terminal, I spotted something out of the corner of my eye. I turned to see a large, black, human-like creature fly up and into the sky. I saw this creature for about four seconds before he flew up and above the cockpit window and out of sight. I immediately shouted it out to my co-pilot, who caught a glimpse of it before it flew out of sight. We were both awestruck by this sighting and it left us dumbfounded. I radioed the incident to the [air traffic control], who made a note of the incident. The rest of the flight was uneventful and we disembarked our passengers without incident. I brought this incident up among colleagues online and was told by several other pilots that they had either seen or heard from others who have seen the exact same thing that we saw.

Early July 2020, at O'Hare Airport (from an air traffic controller):

I was walking toward one of the terminal buildings when I noticed some movement out of the corner of my eye. I stopped and turned in the direction of the movement and noticed a large, black shape coming to a rest on the ground near a light pole. This thing was at least six to seven feet tall and jet black, it looked like a very big bat but was also very human-like in appearance. I noticed that it sported a very large and impressive set of black membranous wings that also looked like the wings of a bat, they were open to their full length and must have been at least 12 feet from tip to tip. The arms on this thing were very long and very skinny, and ended in long bony fingers tipped with what appeared to be long talons. The legs on the being were comparable with the arms, long and skinny, but I was unable to really look at the feet to see if they were also shaped similarly to the hands. I stood there and saw this thing for about 30 seconds as it seemingly looked around the ground. In the time I was looking no fewer than two others had come down the walkway and also saw it. If it had looked up, it would have clearly seen us all staring in bewilderment at it. It kept its head down, looking at the ground until an approaching service vehicle seemingly startled it and it looked up. That is where I saw that its head was short and squat, but had a pair of piercing red eyes. It looked in the direction of the approaching vehicle and then began to flap its wings and took to the air. It disappeared above the building in the span of one to two seconds and was gone out of sight.

As you might have noticed, most of the witnesses are credible professionals who each, apparently, had an encounter with a similar creature. There are hundreds of such reports, with a few even detailing sightings of multiple Mothmen. It sounds as if the population might be growing, now that they've settled in along Lake Michigan's eerie coast.

THE MICHIGAN DOGMAN

It's said that along the shores and forests of Michigan—and possibly Wisconsin too—there roams a terrifying beast that's described as a ferocious-looking half-man/half-wolf creature. Some have likened it to a werewolf, and it's sighted more often in the state than its rival cryptid Bigfoot. It's usually described as six or seven feet tall when standing, with a human-like torso and the head of a wolf or giant dog. Its eyes are a fiery amber, reflect light and seem to glow in the dark, although some reports have mentioned icy-blue eyes. It has large fangs, is capable of moving with great speed and can walk on two or four legs, although it's usually spotted upright.

The first reports of Dogman surfaced in 1887 in Wexford County, Michigan, when two lumberjacks had a frightening encounter in the woods with the creature. Although they escaped unscathed, horses across the area soon began to turn up dead, surrounded by massive paw prints. Oddly, the horses weren't mauled, but instead appeared to have died from fright. In most cases, Dogman seems to have little interest in causing harm; confrontations usually end with the beast skulking away into the night, albeit sometimes departing with a horrifying howling scream that will forever haunt those who hear it. However, he is sometimes seen eating roadkill, and a few reports of nearby animal mutilations have surfaced. Perhaps most chillingly, several witnesses claim that Dogman "smiled" at them, twisting his grizzled muzzle into an evil grin before disappearing into the woods.

Over the years, reports of the bipedal canid have come in waves. In fact, some cryptozoologists believe that Dogman appears in ten-year cycles, in years ending with "7." If that is true, however, the creature must be very busy in his "on" years, since it seems that practically everyone in northern and western Michigan has either had a personal sighting or knows someone else who has. Indeed, the fearsome cryptid seems as endemic to the state as the frighteningly voracious mosquitos that torture residents and tourists alike during the hot summer months.

But Michigan isn't its only home. A Dogman-esque creature has also been spotted in Wisconsin on the back roads near the Sturgeon Bay Ship Canal. A young family from Chicago were headed for a vacation in Door County and took a wrong turn off the highway near Sturgeon Bay. As they drove down a narrow, deserted road near the canal, the car's headlights caught movement in the surrounding brush. Thinking that it was a deer about to jump in their path, the driver hit the brakes. What stepped onto the road, however, was no deer. It looked like a very large, somewhat shaggy gray wolf, but with the body of a man. As they watched, it turned and snarled with a deep rumbling growl. With that, it rose to its hind legs, stared menacingly at the frightened occupants for a moment and then turned and walked back into the trees. Its gait was steady, as if bipedal movement was its norm, although its upper back appeared hunched. As it disappeared into the night, the woods reverberated with a loud snarling howl. The family was terrified, but they feared ridicule, so they didn't speak about it for years.

Another likely relative of Dogman is Wisconsin's infamous Beast of Bray Road, sometimes called the Wisconsin Werewolf. Like Dogman, the creature is said to be six to seven feet tall and usually bipedal, possessing a fur-covered but human-like body, with the head of a giant wolf or dog. It was originally reported in 1936 on a sleepy farm lane named Bray Road, just outside the town of Elkhorn and about fifty miles from Lake Michigan's western shore. In the 1980s, sightings surged, with some people claiming that it swiped at their car with its massive paws as they passed, leaving long scratches in the paint. Since then, it has been spotted in numerous locations across central and southern Wisconsin. The beast gained such notoriety that it spawned a horror film, a documentary, a book and several appearances in episodes of paranormal television shows.

So, what are these creatures? Skeptics claim that they're nothing more than large wild dogs or possibly wolf-dog hybrids. Others suggest the possibility of bears with mange. However, it's pretty hard to imagine that there have been wandering packs of massive bipedal wolf-dogs roaming a multi-state area since the late 1800s. Could it be hoaxes or mass hysteria? Possibly, but most of the witnesses are credible, and evidence such as the impossibly large canid tracks is hard to fake, and least on a widespread and diverse scale.

However, beasts such as this aren't uncommon in Native American mythology. The Chippewa and Odawa tribes that are indigenous to the area talk about a creature that was half man and half dog, and most tribes have beliefs about shapeshifters, humans who can transform at will into other animals, most commonly wolves or bears. Some folks have speculated that Dogman bears some similarity to the First Nation's wendigo (also spelled "windigo"), a fearsome evil spirit that feasts on human flesh and is said to roam Canada and the Great Lakes region, including Michigan. But pinning down what the wendigo looks like is difficult. Although he is sometimes depicted as very much like Dogman, other legends speak of a tall, skeletal, humanoid creature, yet still others show him as a hideous horned beast. Native American author Basil H. Johnston once described the wendigo as "gaunt to the point of emaciation, its desiccated skin pulled tightly over its bones. With its bones pushing out over its skin, its complexion the ash gray of death, and its eyes pushed back deep into the sockets, the Wendigo looked like a gaunt skeleton recently disinterred from the grave. What lips it had were tattered and bloody....Unclean and suffering from suppurations of the flesh, the Wendigo gave off a strange and eerie odor of decay and decomposition, of death and corruption."

From Johnston's description, the wendigo and Dogman definitely sound like two different entities, but they apparently stalk the same territories. Whether the sightings are of Dogman, a werewolf, the wendigo or a shapeshifter, you might use a little caution if you decide to walk the shores of Lake Michigan at night. You never know what you might encounter.

THE MELON HEADS

The tale of the Melon Heads of Michigan began several decades ago in the deep forests surrounding Saugatuck, near Lake Michigan's eastern coast. According to local legends, several children who were born nearby with hydrocephalus—a condition where cerebrospinal fluid accumulates in the brain and causes an increase in head size—were institutionalized at a hospital known as the Junction Insane Asylum in Allegan County, near the Dorr E. Felt mansion. During their stay, they were experimented on and tortured by a cruel scientist named Dr. Crow, sometimes spelled as "Krohe." He would inject strange potions into their skulls or subject them to radiation, which caused their heads to swell to even larger proportions. These experiments caused them great suffering and turned them into terrifying creatures. At some point, the starving and nearly feral mutant children either killed and ate the doctor and escaped or were released into the woods to survive on their own, depending on which version you believe. Now, there are a few problems with the story. For starters, the Allegan County Historical Society insists that an asylum never existed in the area. However, over the years, the twelve-thousand-square-foot Felt mansion and its outbuildings housed a Catholic seminary and boarding school, served as a convent for cloistered nuns, acted as a headquarters for the state police and eventually became a minimum-security adult prison, until the building was abandoned in 1991 and fell into deep disrepair. Proponents of the Melon Head tale have theorized that the children were held captive during one of those periods of the mansion's history, even though it was never officially an asylum. However, there's one other problem with the legend: the nearly identical tale shows up in folklore in Ohio and Connecticut, even including the same evil Dr. Crow.

In any case, the Michigan Melon Heads were well known in the area, even inspiring a 2011 film, appropriately titled *The Melonheads*. Apparently, the mutants returned to live in the derelict mansion in the 1990s, and thrill-seekers who ventured onto the property at night reported catching glimpses of them darting about, seeing curtains move and hearing mumbled voices and heavy breathing. Once restoration of the estate began in the early 2000s, they scattered to hide in various cave systems and tunnels throughout the area, attacking any person unfortunate enough to cross their path.

At this time, the carefully restored Felt estate serves as an elegant event center and historic landmark. The Melon Heads are said to still hide deep in the woods, although sightings are less frequent now. However, one of the Allegan County Historical Society's board members has a more likely—but much more prosaic—explanation for the origin of the Melon Heads, saying that the tale originated as a derogatory nickname for the wealthy students who attended the seminary school: "The town folk referred to them as Melon Heads because they were considered smarter; it was a negative obviously, [as] they thought they came from money and that they were rich and had big heads."

So, are there really small bulbous-headed homicidal maniacs roaming the woods around Saugatuck? And what about the parallel legends in Ohio and Connecticut? Either Dr. Crow was a very busy mad scientist or these creatures are just another iteration of long-standing and widespread folklore.

The *Rouse Simmons*, also known as the "Christmas Tree Ship," hauled freshly cut evergreens from the Northwoods to Chicago each November in time for the Christmas season. On its final voyage in 1912, one crewman refused to sail and took a train home, saying that he was overcome with a sense of dread. It went down with all hands lost.

The *O.S. McFarland* was hauling coal from Erie, Pennsylvania, to Port Washington, Wisconsin, when its captain, George R. Donner, went to his cabin to rest. The crew later discovered that he was missing, although his cabin was locked from the inside.

Left: The *J.H. Hartzell* was a wooden cargo schooner that ran aground on rocks offshore of Frankfort, Michigan, in 1880. Although its entire crew was safely evacuated, they inexplicably left behind their female cook, lashed to a mast in the storm.

Below: The *Carl D. Bradley*, a lake freighter known as the "Queen of the Lakes," suddenly split in two during a storm. Out of a crew of thirty-three, only two survived to tell the tale.

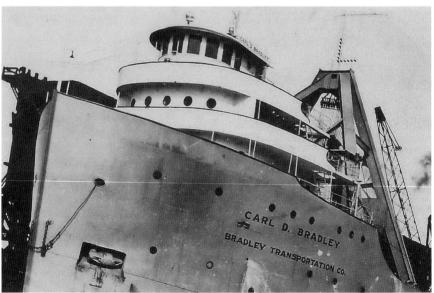

Archaeologists discovered a primitive stone structure deep under the waters of Lake Michigan, including a boulder carved with an image of the long-extinct mastodon. It's believed to date back more than ten thousand years. The inset shows a tracing of the carving, which is difficult to see in underwater photography.

The petroglyph on an ancient boulder under Lake Michigan is enhanced here so the viewer can visualize it more clearly.

In 1953, an F-89C Scorpion jet like these pictured scrambled from Kinross Air Force Base to make contact with an unidentified flying object picked up on Air Defense Command radar. The aircraft and pilot were never seen again.

Although most UFO sightings can be accounted for as misidentified aircraft or natural phenomena, a disturbing number of credible sightings remain unexplained.

In 1978, four U.S. Coast Guard stations, including the one at Two Rivers, Wisconsin, observed a strange cigar-shaped craft zigzagging at tremendous speed across the skies of Lake Michigan over a period of several hours. Pictured here is the harbor at Two Rivers.

Meteors are sometimes mistaken for UFOs, but not all sightings can be explained so easily.

Waugoshance Lighthouse is one of forty-four lighthouses in Lake Michigan. It is rumored to be haunted by the ghost of a missing keeper.

Fata Morgana is an optical phenomenon (mirage) that takes place when light bends through air layers of different temperatures. It sometimes occurs on Lake Michigan and distorts objects or their apparent location in a manner that can appear supernatural.

The woods surrounding the lake are said to be home to various cryptids, including Dogman, Bigfoot and the Mothman.

Poverty Island has been cursed with misfortune, but it might also be the home to $400 million in gold.

ASSORTED ODDITIES

Oddity, like beauty, is in the eye of the beholder.
What one person rejects as lunacy, another reveres as truth.
—*Philip Gulley, author*

Although this book has compiled many of the terrible disasters and fearsome incidents that gave the Lake Michigan Triangle its foreboding reputation, not all of the strange happenings have been disastrous. Some were just, well, strange. Here are a few of the stories behind unexplained and odd events and bizarre phenomena that make folks wonder if the region is indeed controlled by mysterious forces—or if fact truly is stranger than fiction.

THE MISSING MONTHS OF STEVEN KUBACKI

Hope College is a private Christian four-year liberal arts college in Holland, Michigan, not far from the shores of Lake Michigan. It was founded in 1851 by Dutch immigrants and is affiliated with the Reformed Church in America (RCA), a Protestant denomination. With just slightly more than three thousand students, it's a small but picturesque campus with strong conservative values. It's also considered one of the top liberal arts colleges in the state, and it attracts many of the best and brightest students to its halls.

In 1978, one such student was a twenty-three-year-old German and history major by the name of Steven Kubacki. Another student enrolled at the same time as Kubacki described him as "brilliant" and a "little more free-spirited" than some of his peers. He was known as a skilled outdoorsman and had spent time mountain-climbing while studying abroad in Europe, where he'd left behind a German girlfriend when he returned to his studies in the United States. His life was going exactly according to plan; he was nearing graduation and already had a job lined up with the *Holland Sentinel* newspaper. His future certainly looked bright.

On the bitterly cold and windy Saturday afternoon of February 18, 1978, Kubacki decided to get outside for some exercise and fresh air. He bundled up appropriately to face the frigid weather and told people he was planning on doing some cross-country skiing along the Lake Michigan beach. It was something he had done many times before, and he was definitely quite familiar with the area. As the hours passed with no sign of his return, though, his friends grew increasingly concerned. Thinking that perhaps he was staying with others on campus, they waited until the next day, but he never showed up. That afternoon, his roommate called the authorities to report him as missing. It seems that the police might have been slow to react, probably figuring that he was off partying somewhere and would soon return home, hung over and apologetic. The following day, however, snowboarders came across an abandoned backpack and a pair of skis and poles in the snow near the frozen shoreline; they belonged to Steven. Suddenly, it became obvious that this wasn't a typical college bender, and thus began an intensive air and ground search that included helicopters and tracking dogs. The only clue they had was a set of footprints, leading ominously out onto the partially frozen ice on the lake's surface for about two hundred feet, where they abruptly ended. Although Michigan State Police stopped short of declaring that Kubacki had drowned, a trooper noted, "There's a very strong current in the area and much of the ice is broken and piled up…[it's] an unsafe place to go."

After weeks of fruitless searching, it was generally assumed that the student had fallen through the ice and was dead. That spring, Hope College awarded him a Bachelor of Arts degree in absentia. He had only been nine credits short of graduation at the time of his disappearance. His parents, however, still held out hope that he was alive and that there was another explanation. Apparently, they weren't alone. The detectives working the case actually sent Steven's dental records to investigators in Chicago on the off chance that he might be among the unidentified victims of serial killer John Wayne Gacy, who had tortured and killed at least thirty-three young men before his arrest in December 1978. Unlike Kubacki's parents, detectives didn't believe that there was a chance that he was still alive, but they wanted to be certain they didn't have a homicide on their hands. They were able to verify that he hadn't fallen prey to Gacy, but with no sign of a body, they were no closer to understanding what had happened that February afternoon. That is, until the answer came to them more than a year later.

On the cool and sunny afternoon of May 5, 1979, Steven woke up in a grassy field. He was more than seven hundred miles away from Michigan, in the town of Pittsfield, Massachusetts, and everything around him— including the clothes he wore—seemed unfamiliar. A backpack lying next to him contained maps and receipts showing that he had traveled to Sacramento, San Francisco, Reno, Chicago and Utah. Also packed neatly inside were sneakers and a T-shirt from a marathon in Wisconsin. He remembered none of this. In his pocket was forty dollars in cash. Confused and disoriented, he stumbled to his feet and walked to a nearby newsstand to pick up a newspaper. His last memory was of being on the Lake Michigan shoreline in the freezing darkness, feeling lost and frightened. How could he now be in Massachusetts, nearly fifteen months later? He wasn't unfamiliar with the state; in fact, it was his home. His aunt lived less than twenty miles to the south of Pittsfield in Great Barrington, and his parents lived in South Deerfield, about forty-five miles to the east. Steven made his way to his aunt's home, where he was able to reunite with the rest of his family.

Shortly thereafter, a local divinity student who saw the news about the miraculous reappearance reported that he had picked up a hitchhiker that very day who said his name was Nathan and who asked to be driven to a house in Great Barrington. "Nathan" had said that he was visiting a friend to deliver news about a missing mutual acquaintance. Of course, the student later identified the hitchhiker as Steven, and the house he was dropped at was his aunt's. Why would Kubacki bother making up such an odd story? And where had he been?

Although some folks, including the police and college officials, suspected that the whole disappearance had been staged, Kubacki's friends vehemently denied the possibility. They claimed he seemed happy and excited about the future and showed no signs of being capable of such deceit. His parents didn't care what had happened. They were just overjoyed to have him back. For his part, Steven insisted that the story was true and claimed that he had no reason to disappear. He refused psychiatric care, saying that he was mentally sound, and blamed his "blackout" on exhaustion.

If this story isn't already strange enough, there's a postscript. *The Anchor*, the student newspaper of Hope College, published a story on October 30, 2020, titled "Michigan Triangle Claims Another Victim." The fictional report details the supposed disappearance of another student, which closely resembles (and frequently references) Kubacki's missing time. It places the blame squarely on aliens, the Lake Michigan Triangle and government coverups. Satire? So they claim.

THE TRAGEDY AND TREASURE OF POVERTY ISLAND

Poverty Island is a small, uninhabited, windswept outcropping of rock and trees situated between Michigan's Garden Peninsula and Wisconsin's Door Peninsula. At only 192 acres, it's one of the smaller islands in the Grand Traverse chain, but its position between Big Bay de Noc and Green Bay placed it directly in the path of late nineteenth-century and early twentieth-century shipping lanes. In 1865, a railroad line went into service between Escanaba and the inland iron ore mines, turning Little Bay de Noc into a bustling port. During the day, ships could sail the more direct northern passage between Poverty Island and Gull Island by visually weaving past the dangerous rocks, but at night, with no light to safely guide them, they were forced to take the longer and more circuitous southern route. Faced with the volume of traffic, the Lighthouse Board went before Congress in 1867 to plead for money to build a lighthouse on Poverty Island. The estimated cost was $18,000, but the funding wasn't approved until 1873. Almost immediately, the trouble began.

Two months after work commenced in August of that year, an unexplained fire broke out and roared through the workers' temporary living quarters. It also destroyed much of the remaining building material, putting an end to construction for the year. The next spring, they began work once more, but the fire had left them short of material and out of money. Once again they had to stop, although before they departed, they managed to affix a temporary light to the partially built tower. Congress approved an additional $3,000 the following year, and the structure was finally completed and topped with a permanent lantern room in August 1875. More than eight years after the initial request, Poverty Island Lighthouse officially entered service.

Unfortunately, within a few years, the tower showed severe cracking and settling due to shoddy workmanship, and it required major repairs. To prevent further damage, the Lighthouse Board ordered that a retaining wall be added to stop some of the shifting and shore up the foundation. And although the light had made the passage much safer, it didn't solve all of the problems. In June 1884, the steamship *Oscar Townsend* tried to blindly navigate between the islands one intensely foggy dark night. Instead, it ran aground on Gull Island, causing $7,200 in damages to its hull—nearly $250,000 today—and spilling some of its cargo of ore. Immediately, newspapers and mariners blamed the Lighthouse Board for failing to erect a fog signal. The board moved swiftly, and by the end of the next season, Poverty Island was sporting a fancy new ten-inch steam whistle, fueled by coal and wood that was loaded into the attached boiler by the hardworking keepers. On average, they needed to fire it up about three hundred hours per year due to the seemingly omnipresent mist.

However, it appeared that bad luck swirled around the lighthouse just as frequently as the fog. In 1912, head keeper James McCormick took the station's small launch to Escanaba to pick up some essentials. On his return trip, the boat inexplicably caught fire. The *Escanaba Morning Press* reported the story in some detail: "McCormick worked as long as he could to try and gain control of the flames and then finding that they were gaining headway rapidly, and that the tiny craft was doomed, he seized a life preserver and jumped over the side of the boat into the water. After drifting about for a considerable length of time he was picked up by a passing steamer and taken to his home on Poverty Island. The gasoline launch burned to the water's edge and then sank."

After McCormick retired in 1915, he was replaced by Niels Jensen, and things were mostly peaceful for a while. But in early 1923, Jensen and his two assistant keepers, William Lee and Benjamin Johnson, were busy preparing for the upcoming season. Lee's family home was on Washington Island, although his wife and children would spend summers with him on Poverty Island. Early one June afternoon, he headed to Washington Island to pick them up. When they returned to the station, Lee mentioned that he didn't feel well, and he went inside to rest. After a short time, his wife went in to check on him and found him dead on the floor from an apparent heart attack. While Jensen attended to the grieving widow, he asked his other assistant, Benjamin Johnson, to take Lee's body to Washington Island so that funeral preparations could begin. They only had one boat, and Jensen didn't want the wife and children to suffer through the twenty-mile trip with Lee's dead body. Once the corpse was safely with the undertaker, Johnson would return to fetch the family and bring them back home.

Johnson set off on his mission, with his dead friend and colleague wrapped in blankets beside him. But first, he stopped at St. Martin Island Lighthouse to ask them to send help to Poverty Island, since Jensen was now working alone. Unfortunately, by the time he was able to continue his trip, night had crept in along with a heavy fog, and in the murky darkness, he ran aground on a reef. Luckily, the boat wasn't significantly damaged, but he was forced to spend a very cold and eerie night, alone with a corpse and stranded in the middle of the foreboding, foggy lake, until daylight came and he was able to free the craft.

In 1936, head keeper Jensen would also fall victim to the seemingly cursed island. After spending twenty-one years at the station—quite impressive for a job that entailed back-breaking labor and long periods of isolation—he was attending a school board meeting on Washington Island and was struck and killed by an automobile as he walked to the building. For a man who spent his life facing danger on the water, it seemed ironic that he'd meet his end on a rural roadway.

Despite all the troubles and tragedies, however, there's a persistent legend that Poverty Island might also hold the secret to tremendous wealth. The story begins during the latter part of the American Civil War. At that time, the Confederate army was running short on cash and desperate to replenish its war chest. The CSA reached out to French emperor Napoleon Bonaparte for help. France was then a major consumer of American cotton, and Bonaparte feared that the flow of cotton might stop if the South lost the war. He agreed to cough up some funding, in the form of nearly $400 million in gold bullion and coins. The plan was to send the loot through Canada, where it could be loaded onto a ship and sailed down the St. Lawrence River to Lake Michigan, secretly unloaded in Chicago and smuggled down to Confederate headquarters. But once again, Lake Michigan showed no mercy. Depending on which version you believe, the schooner was either smashed on the rocks by the waves, attacked by pirates or gunned down by Union forces, but somehow the chests of gold wound up in the water immediately offshore of Poverty Island. There were said to be five chests, all chained together. Most people considered the tale to be fictitious, just one of those stories that grizzled old seamen tell over a shot of whiskey.

That is, until 1929, when a passing ship ran aground on the island. As a tugboat worked to free it, the anchor snagged something heavy. When the crew finally dragged it to the surface, they saw that it was pulling up what appeared to be a string of chests. But before they could get a closer look, the chain snapped and sent the objects tumbling back into the murky water. Despite repeated attempts, they couldn't dredge them up again. A few years later, Karl Jessen, the son of Poverty Island assistant lighthouse keeper Abraham Jessen, was relaxing on the shore and watching a storm roll in when he noticed a salvage boat, the *Captain Lawrence*, working in the channel. Suddenly, he heard yelling and cheering across the water and saw men running excitedly across the deck. Jessen wondered if they had discovered the lost gold. Almost immediately, however, the storm hit and the winds kicked up with a brutal fury, lifting the small ship on the waves and smashing it against the rocks. It seemed that Lake Michigan didn't want to give up its treasure just yet. Although the crew was able to reach the safety of the lighthouse, their ship was a complete loss, and they never spoke a word of the gold.

Since then, divers and salvage crews have unsuccessfully combed the water, hoping to find the treasure. They did discover the remains of the *Captain Lawrence* in 1993, but there was no sign of the chests. Is there a fortune in gold on Poverty Island, or is it just a colorful legend? The controversy goes on, but only the lake knows for sure.

SAILING IN A VORTEX

There are plenty of weird reports of anomalies on Lake Michigan, but many of them are stories that have been passed down over the years or long-ago interviews of questionable accuracy. One of the eeriest, however, is a first-person account from a blog post by author and sailing enthusiast Kathy Doore. Her words were captured by writer Ellen Killoran, in her newsletter *Cold Dead Hands* via Substack:

> *Not an hour out of port and quite unexpectedly, a dense fog rapidly descended upon us.... The winds were erratic, filling the mainsail from two opposing directions....I leaned over the rail and looked at the surface of the lake. It was calm with little movement. Strangely, a few seconds later as I righted myself, I found I was extremely cold.*
>
> *I turned toward the helm to ask my crew mates if they too were cold and to my utter astonishment they were no longer standing next to me.... Dumbfounded, I called out and located them standing up on the aft deck, where it was several degrees warmer. They seemed perplexed, and urged me to join them. That's when I noticed that no one was steering the boat.*

> *The Captain raised his arms high over his head, gleefully wiggling his hands and fingers in the air, and stated he hadn't been steering for the past ten minutes. Yet, not one minute before, I was certain he had been standing next to me at the helm.*
>
> *Draped in dense fog, the vessel began a curious aquatic dance. Slowly, but deliberately, she turned on her axis completing three perfect 360-degree pirouettes, without ever crossing the wind. Then, just as suddenly as it had appeared, the fog vanished. To our utter astonishment, we saw the other two boats all within a few hundred yards of each other, rotating in exactly the same manner.*

Later, Doore also spoke about this strange occurrence with a reporter from the *Chicago Tribune*. She claimed that when they returned to port, they were unable to account for several hours. "Missing time" is often a hallmark of UFO encounters, although Doore never mentioned seeing any strange lights. Just an otherworldly, ghostly fog that enveloped everything around it and spirited away time. She said that once her experience went public, she was deluged by reports from others who claimed to have witnessed similar phenomena in the waters off Chicago. "There is a long history of anomalous phenomena in Lake Michigan," she acknowledged.

Weirdness Under the Water

One of the most exciting recent additions to Lake Michigan Triangle lore was the 2007 discovery of what was billed as the "Lake Michigan Stonehenge." Dr. Mark Holley, an underwater archaeologist and teacher at Northwestern Michigan College, was part of a group that was researching shipwrecks in Grand Traverse Bay through the use of side-scan sonar when they spotted a strange anomaly. Holley and other divers went down to investigate, and they found a mile-long line of stones, including a large boulder that appears to have a petroglyph of a mastodon carved into it. Mastodons were large elephant-like animals that went extinct more than ten thousand years ago, so it was likely that this site had been created before the retreating glaciers carved out Lake Michigan.

Almost immediately, the media was awash with stories about a great stonehenge practically under our feet! Why travel all the way to England when we have the same thing here in the Midwest? Except…it's not quite the same. Holley was frustrated by the misinformation surrounding his find and tried to set the record straight: "[T]here is not a henge associated with the site and the individual stones are relatively small when compared to what most people think of as European standing stones. It should be clearly understood that this is not a megalith site like Stonehenge…the site in Grand Traverse Bay is best described as a long line of stones which is over a mile in length." He believes that the formation might have been used by prehistoric hunters to drive caribou, and another researcher has since discovered a similar structure under Lake Huron.

Okay, so it's not another megalith like Stonehenge, but an ancient carving of a mastodon on a massive boulder and a mile-long course of stones carefully set in place by prehistoric hunters, sitting deep under the waves of Lake Michigan? That's still pretty exciting.

But ancient carvings aren't the only oddity on the lake floor. In roughly twenty feet of water, about eight hundred feet from shore in Little Traverse Bay, there's an 1,800-pound Italian marble statue of Jesus Christ on the cross resting in the sand. It's about eleven feet long, and you can only see it if you're in scuba gear. Well, except for a few frigid days in the dead of winter, when the Little Traverse Bay Dive Club carves a hole in the ice, sets up a tent and invites the public to trudge on over and take a peek.

You might wonder how it got there. It's a rather complicated and heartbreaking story. In the early 1960s, Gerald Schapinski, a farmer's son from Bad Axe, Michigan, was tragically killed when a rifle he had just gotten for his fifteenth birthday went off accidentally and killed him. His grieving parents purchased the massive effigy to be placed on his grave, but when it arrived from Europe, one of the arms was broken off. The sculptor in Italy agreed to replace it, leaving the broken one in the hands of the insurance company, which put it up for auction. At that point, a dive club in Wyandotte bought it, repaired the arm and dropped it into the bay to honor divers who have lost their lives in the sport. It was originally much farther from shore and in deeper water, but by 1985, wave patterns had begun to deposit heavy amounts of silt over it. When they attempted to relocate it, the other arm broke off, and it was a few years until it could once again be restored. Since 1986, the statue has rested in its current home just offshore of Petoskey, where it serves as a unique landmark and a testament to the inherent dangers of diving Lake Michigan.

ABOUT THE AUTHOR

Gayle Soucek is an author, historian and freelance editor with more than a dozen books and numerous magazine articles to her credit, including *Haunted Door County*; *Door County Tales: Shipwrecks, Cherries and Goats on the Roof*; and *Chicago Calamities: Disaster in the Windy City*. Gayle and her photographer husband divide their time between their home in a Chicago suburb and a second home in Gills Rock, Wisconsin, directly overlooking the Death's Door passage. It's this proximity to the rich history and unexplained events that occur along the Lake Michigan shoreline that inspired this book on the Lake Michigan Triangle.

Visit us at
www.historypress.com